LO&VE
DEATH
IN A QUEER UNIVERSE

Caffyn Jesse

EcstaticBelonging.com

LOVE AND DEATH IN A QUEER UNIVERSE

A Note on the Practices

There is a well-known biological principle: too much stress is harmful. It literally biophysically damages cells, and impairs the functioning of nervous systems. And too-little stress is just as harmful; it leads to nervous system atrophy. There is a place of just-right stress that supports the growth and strength of any organism. I call it our personal neural learning zone. The same principle applies in our relationships with one another. There is a place of just-enough stress that is our interpersonal learning zone, where we can be in the embodied learning of even-better love. If you engage with any of the practices and exercises I offer here, please honour your own learning zone. Any particular exercise can feel too dangerous, making it impossible for learning to emerge. Or any exercise can feel too boring to foster nervous system growth. Readers may have disabilities that make an exercise irrelevant. Exercises can be done in your imagination, or actually. Imagining doing something new lights up new neural pathways and generates neuroplastic change.

Cover image: Earth, Sun and Moon align
in an eclipse, image by Ipicgr from Pixabay

Paperback ISBN: 978-0-9738332-8-7
EPUB ISBN: 978-0-9738332-9-4

Book Layout: Ravi Ramgati

TABLE OF CONTENTS

Introductory Images

INTRODUCTION

IN A NUTSHELL

SCIENCE AND SACRED INTIMACY

I am growing old in a culture that sees no reason for it. Science tries to find a cure for it. Anti-aging industries try to reverse it. Diet and exercise regimes try to postpone it. Social worlds show contempt for it. There is no value in increased frailty, eccentricity, and non-functionality. Old is unlovable. I began this book with my own aching inquiry.

> Can I learn to grow old and die
> in ways that truly welcome and
> accommodate aging and death?
> Can my increasing vulnerability
> become a guide, instead of something to hide?

Reading stories of western science is one way I tune into older, wiser parts of me. Since the particles and energies of me began with the birth of the universe, what does the stardust of me know, that my brain is unaware of? What do earth, moon and old-growth forests have to teach me, about growing old in enduring love? Understanding metabolic processes in cells, and signalling molecules in nervous systems and ecosystems, means I can sit at the feet of my biological elders, and listen to their stories.

I read science through the lens of a sacred intimate. It is my job and vocation to share whole-body touch and embodied love. In the weave of science and sacred intimacy, I find the universe has much to teach us, about how we might age ecstatically, and die consciously, in love with each other and the planet. In integrating science into my inquiry, I'm not trying to discern the truth, as if there were an objective truth outside us. I'm trying to discern how stories from science serve as truing mechanisms. What ways of knowing atoms, cells and stars guide us to grow old and die in love, practising gratitude, peace, courage and ecstasy?

Writing this book, I wrote myself into a new relationship with the world. I have come to live in a universe where all the molecules of us tell stories. They joke and jostle, and they want to be heard. Ecosystems and biosphere hold and scold us. Systems of life-giving love that emerged through billions of years of learning go on emerging, within and around us. A vast network of interwoven systems exists through me and you. As I learn to listen to the reciprocal network, I can join it, and add my awareness to the multitudes of awarenesses it integrates and inspires.

This book is meant to be fun. I embrace my own silliness. Having never formally studied science, I roam playfully in the realms of quantum physics and cell biology. I find sweet metaphors and compelling stories in the lives and loves of plants and animals, and the quantum entanglements of subatomic particles. My focus on walking the path of embodied love, as I grow old, yields spirited solutions to scientific mysteries.

At the same time, this book is a serious inquiry into how we can grow old and die in love together, as the world ends. With social crises and ecological catastrophes pushing the biosphere beyond repair, what consciousness cultivation and death preparation practices might possibly matter? Listening to the love stories of the universe, I find ways we can choose to live and die that make a difference.

THE PATIENT PRACTICE OF LOVE

I share very personal stories in this book, about my own pathways to love and belonging. I will never belong in the world of normative belonging; there are so many ways I transgress rules, laws, and social norms. And yet, in the relational world I am blessed to live in, we are finding and forging a better belonging. Through my work and play as a sacred intimate, I am part of co-creating a relational matrix where my individuation, and yours, can flourish. We can help each other grow neurological capacities for resourced independence and courageous interdependence. We can share and cultivate ecstatic experiences, interwoven with ordinary life.

I know that I could not be me without the patient practice of love. Cultivating a relational matrix wherein we fully and freely practice love is my great passion. In my counternormative life, my chosen family, and the communities of practice I am a part of, we engage in radical work and play that meets my deepest longing for belonging. I want to discern, celebrate and share the magic, with thanks to the precious human and nonhuman relationships I find belonging in. I write this book to affirm and amplify the love we are making. I write to invite you, dear reader, to share this love and co-create. I write because writers were my first relational matrix. If as a child I had not found writing by counternormative, critical thinkers, and poets of the extraordinary, I would not have grown old.

When I began this book, I didn't know how my own aging and dying could belong, in a world where aging and death seem so unlovable and unloved. What I found through writing, and now I feel in the cells and soul of me, is a giddy gladness of amplified belonging.

> I have learned to belong to my own process
> of aging and dying, and belong to all the ways
> I resist it by trying to last a little longer,
> and make even more love.

There is a web of belonging that is ever-emerging, in the tiniest subatomic particles of us, through the whole biosphere. It is made manifest through my own receiving of it, and through my finding ways to share it with you.[1]

IN A NUTSHELL

This is a long book about my life and learning. If you don't have time to read it, here it is in a nutshell:

> Let's delight in difference,
> and tend to rupture with repair,
> so we can reach for rapture.
> Let's keep going there.

There's a science to it, if you care. It's a way of being that our molecules all share. There's a weave of life and death that our cells know. There's a song the whole earth sings. It's a beautiful song. Let's sing along.

---

1 For more sharing of the web of belonging, please see my book *Ecstatic Belonging* and join me in the free online learning environment I offer at EcstaticBelonging.com.

CHAPTER I

RELATIONSHIP ADVICE FROM STARDUST

SINGULARITY (BADLY BEHAVED & INFINITE)

In mathematics, the word "singularity" describes the point at which a mathematical object becomes badly behaved. There are no easy answers, and the question itself becomes nonsense. One divided by zero generates a singularity; the answer is infinite. In physics, a "singularity" emerges as two things with mass converge. The force of gravity – centred in the centre of each thing with mass – increases as things get closer and closer. If differences don't collide, break apart and scatter each other, then gravity gets stronger and stronger in the diminishing space between them. At the point where there is no more space between two centres, gravity becomes infinite. A point of zero size has infinite density, and a singularity is born.

My storytelling is not about math or physics. My focus is intimacy and individuation. In my world, "singularity" refers to the misbehaving mystery and irrevocable fact of our uniqueness. What a challenge, and a miracle, that we are singular beings.

Each one of us is unique, and we are strange to one another. For me, the singularities described by math and physics are potent metaphors. I like to hold them in my mind, as I contemplate the singularity each one of us is, and what new singularities we might find and forge as we grow old together in embodied love.

The world of normative belonging is so unloving. Love that really wants and welcomes us – love that can really feel and find us – is rare and precious. Working as a paid practitioner of sacred intimacy makes space in my daily routine, and in my cells and soul, where I co-create everyday experiences of embodied love. Sacred intimates are whores whose work is deeply intimate and profoundly sacred. Where others hope and wait for love, and fear they will never find it, we make love. There is a technology.

We make love with tender, exciting, whole body touch that impacts neurochemistry and endocrine function. We touch to contradict self-loathing, soothe the effects of trauma, and replace the imprints of painful, unwanted touch with pleasurable, respectful touch of toes, ears, scars and thighs. We love peoples' minds by coaxing communication, and honoring each person in their desires, while honoring our own boundaries. Offering each person we touch our unconditional positive regard, we invite new neural pathways linking brain with heart, pelvis, voice and feeling. We love peoples' spirits. I feel my own spirit soar, as I greet yours with wonder and amazement. We connect emotionally, and offer love as one wounded human being to another. Riding waves of emotion, we often travel from deep grief to elation in a single session. We talk and touch at the pace of trust, with care for each person's neural learning zone.

Embodied love emerges with our patient practice. This form of love has nothing to do with scripts for compatibility and social consequence that usually limit what we call love. I've shared loving touch with people old and young, fat and thin, conventionally attractive and not – people I knew well and those I would never see again – and people who spanned the spectrum of genders in the gender galaxy. We don't need to wait to be moved by spontaneous desire to make embodied love; we can simply set aside space and time with intention to invite the erotic in. We don't need to be attractive to each other, or turned on at the same time, to make embodied love. Rather, we can take turns offering each other wanted touch, in ways that let our shy souls safely unfold.

We live in a world that ostensibly values the individual, and yet most people feel isolated and uncertain in their differences from one another. We can become more certain, joyful versions of ourselves, when we feel held in embodied love. Over years spent in a counternormative community of practice with other practitioners, clients and students of sacred intimacy, I saw how the singularity each one of us is can keep on emerging, in in a relational matrix where we consistently, kindly, passionately and compassionately offer each other embodied love. We can keep on becoming the badly-behaved, intricate, infinite singularities we are, while we stay connected in community.

GROWING OLD IN LOVE TOGETHER: FUNDAMENTAL FORCES

To manifest everyday experiences of embodied love, we need to eschew the rules and roles of normative belonging. We can be inspired by the story of the universe. According to the laws of physics, the universe should not exist. The "Big Bang" should have produced matter and antimatter in equal amounts. Matter and antimatter cancel each other out; they destroy each other. And yet we have this queer, counternormative universe, with matter in it. Clearly, the universe itself is a rule-breaker, who figured out how to live long and matter, outside the law.

Physics describes four "fundamental" forces – strong nuclear force, electromagnetic force, weak force and gravity – that govern how particles of matter interact with one another. Fundamental forces emerged in the early universe, as energy figured out how to matter.

Strong nuclear force is an emergent property of relationships between quarks - the tiniest particles of the universe. This is the force that coheres protons and neutrons, and holds atomic nuclei together. It comes into being as quarks gather in groups of three, and continually adjust their states in response to their companions' ever-changing states.

Electromagnetic force holds charged particles together in love affairs with both spaciousness and passion enough to make love last. Particles balance and contain each other's charge, while staying separate enough not to merge. This is the force that coheres atoms, so atoms can have probability fields with edges. Matter has power then, to matter to itself, and feel and follow its desire to matter even more.

The weak force is the power of satisfaction, held inside an atom, as it decays into longing. This force is subtle and slow: weak force is some 10 million times weaker than electromagnetic force. Yet much is empowered by the slow, subtle process of tracking desire, the satisfaction of desire, the savoring of fulfillment, and the ongoing emergence of desire for even more.

Table: The four Fundamental Forces guiding all matter in the universe all come into being as emergent properties of enduring relationships.

Force	Emergent in	Satisfied by	Relative Strength
Strong Force quarks become protons	relationships between quarks within the nucleus of atoms	each particle continually adjusts its state in response to other particles' ever-changing states	Much Stronger
Electromagnetic Force protons and electrons become atoms	relationships between charged particles within atoms	particles balance and contain each other's charge, while staying separate enough not to merge	
Weak Force radioactive decay	aging transforms subatomic particles, neutrons become protons	the decay of satisfaction into desire is neverending	↓
Gravity atoms cohere in communities with mass enough to bend local spacetime	relationships between all bodies with mass	sustainable patterns of enduring relationship between bodies that support both separation and connection	Much weaker

Four Fundamental Forces

Strong Force

binds particles within
the nucleus of atoms

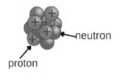

Weak Force

energy generated by
radioactive decay

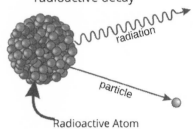

Electromagetic Force

keeps electrons in orbit around
the nucleus of atoms

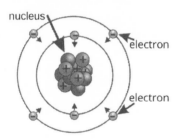

Gravitational Force

binds particles into galaxies,
stars and planets

The universe was already old and wise – a billion years old –
before the force of **gravity** emerged. As particles gathered to share
their new understandings of how to matter, they cohered inside
larger shapes, with edges, mass and density. Strong nuclear
force, electromagnetic force, and weak force could still govern
all kinds of conflict and commotion at the sub-atomic and atomic
level, while the larger community held together, with something

approximating neutrality. High-intensity drama, unfolding in many intricate, intimate ways, didn't have to end things.

In complex communities of particles, the subtle power of gravity became inarguable. Stars were born. Galaxies began to form. Stars grew old, for billions of years, and then they died, exploding in brilliant supernovae. Stardust released in the spectacular death of a nearby supernovae coalesced into our own sun, 4.6 billion years ago. The sun is an aggregation of lighter, older elements of hydrogen and helium. All around the sun, smaller masses of newer, more complicated stardust, born in the death of a great star, met and merged with each other, aggregating into the planets of our solar system.

Listening to the energy of me, aging in lasting loving relationships as the stardust of me, I get guidance for who I want to be. I know better how I want to weave lasting intimacies and co-create communities with those I love. There is so much wisdom in our stardust. Understanding how fundamental forces exist as emergent properties of enduring relationships, I feel my way into more sustainable patterns of loving connection. We co-create fundamental forces in relationships that bind us together in enduring love. We come to matter by finding attunement with each others' ever-changing states, and by giving each other lots of space and time. We generate energy by savouring our satisfactions and letting them evolve into new longings. We make time for living and loving by joining with others in complex community.

BEING THE CENTRE OF THE UNIVERSE

To my delight, I see affinities between the ways the whole wide universe comes to matter, and the ways we matter to one another. Just as each human is both inarguable singularity and host of ever-uncertain possibilities, every quantum of energy is at once discernible certainty and probabilistic cloud. It is only as we are held in each other's awareness, with embodied love, that our energy can cycle and stay awhile. We feel it amplified. If we become centred in our own uniqueness, as those we love stay centred in their uniqueness, we can evolve our singularities together. We feel and find ourselves because we matter to each other. Just as the singularity each one of us is emerges in the experience of embodied love, so it is with the whole universe.

It turns out that each singular observer has a core relationship with the universe. The centre of the universe is me; it is also you. The farther from our own centre we look, the farther back in time we see; light and sound from the birth of the universe is just now arriving, from the most distant parts of the universe. Energy from the beginning of time and space vibrates all the particles of us, at a particular frequency.

> The universe creates and supports us;
> it also wants and needs us.
> We matter to the universe.

> Time and space begin here and now,
> in each of us, in our singular centre.
> They end at the edges of our awareness.
> Particular points emerge from probabilistic clouds
> as our noticing of the universe conjures it into being.

> Without ongoing discernments,
> there would only be only Chaos.
> With shared discernments, there is Eros.
> We have so much to love and cherish, then.
> There is so much we would mourn and miss.

GROWING OLD IN ENDURING LOVE

We are made of quarks, gluons, and leptons. We are stardust, forged from complex elements birthed in the death of a star. The unique being that I am is a distinctive one that unpredictably emerges from the relationship of all my parts, in this moment, through my life, in relationship with unique others. The emergent properties and new possibilities that each of us is, and each loving relationship is, cannot be predicted from the properties of the component parts. Yet principles of self and relationship can be observed at work and play in the behaviours, needs and longings of our tiniest parts and their histories.

At the sub-atomic and atomic level, up to the level of each human being, through the biosphere, to the universe, we find singularities. Individuation is an organizing principle of all matter, within and around us. As we age, we amplify our difference from all that is other. Like every particularity, we need self-satisfaction enough to sustain our difference. We need to feel our personal centre, and follow the momentum and trajectory of our uniqueness.

We simultaneously house the joys of connection and unity: at the sub-atomic level, up to the level of our skins, and in enduring systems of loving relationships. At every level – the subatomic world, the solar system, the nervous system, the biotic community – what is connected is what endures. Without dynamic, stable relationships, there can be no quarks or atoms, no galaxy and star formation, no biosphere, no intimate sphere.

In every sustainable and sustaining relational system, we need to feel welcome and wanted in our difference. The system has to have time and space enough for each particularity to feel and follow the momentum of its differentiation, while it

15

simultaneously feels and follows its attraction to the other and the whole. We can unfold the power and dignity of our uniqueness, inside delighted relationships. We can honour the power and dignity of one another. We can allow our attractions, without collapsing into them. We can find satisfactions and make space to savour. With open-hearted, welcoming, embodied love, we can keep unfolding more delights.

The sorrows of limits, loss, disaggregation and ends are always part of open-hearted love. When a loved one dies, or fails us, when life separates us, or a relationship demands too much sacrifice, we can lose ourselves, or lose our longing for more love. Or we can stretch, so we can keep on evolving our individuation while simultaneously expanding our love for trustworthy others. We can learn to notice where and how we are pulled out of love, or away from differentiation and dignity. We can coach and coax each other, and tease and please each other, and feel what is true and right for us separately and together. Like the stardust we are made of, we can grow old in ever-emerging, enduring love.

EMBODIED PRACTICE:
BE THE CENTRE OF THE UNIVERSE

There is a still, quiet centre that is the centre of you. We perpetually organize our balance around a gravitational centre.

Feel into your personal centre. Feel how your centre shifts and changes as you move and bend. Standing is a balancing act that brings our centre of gravity up into the pelvis. Move in whatever ways are accessible to you. Standing, lying down, bending sideways or rolling around, keep feeling into your personal centre of gravity, and finding your singular centre. Try it with your eyes closed. Can you start to notice a resting reference point for balancing you, where your body doesn't need references from outside itself?

Let your awareness extend from the singular centre of you as you feel into the universe of time and space outside your skin. Send your awareness in every direction, all around you, out to the edge of space and the beginning of time. Look even further, into the timeless time before the beginning of time, where there are entangled histories of many possible universes. From all these universes, use your centre to discern the edge of this particular universe. Without you at the centre, this singular universe could not exist. Want it. Welcome it. Let time and space begin, and extend for 13.8 billion years, still centred in you, right here, right now. Feel how the singularity that is you, and the singularity of this particular universe, are one.

EROTIC PRACTICE: STARS ARE BORN

Set a specific time aside, as a dedicated time-outside-time to explore arousal, alone or with others. Use breath, sound, movement, imagination and touch to amplify erotic charge.

Feel the growing density and immensity of the Eros that is contained in you. Find your ecstatic climax, however that unfolds for you in the given time period (including but not limited to genital orgasm). Notice your climax, in all its particularity, and savour it for as long as you can. Then linger in satisfaction, imagining the scattered particles of you slowly assembling into swirling galaxies of radiant stars.

DEATH PREPARATION PRACTICE: INTENSITY AND IMMENSITY

Light a candle in the dark. Looking at the candle, and the dark, contemplate the idea that being is intensity, while nonbeing is immensity. Feel into the intensity of your own being, centred in the centre of you. Feel how nonbeing presses at the edges of your awareness, the edges of your lifetime, the edges of your skin. Blow out the candle, and notice any remnants of intensity that hover as an afterglow.

REFLECTION: CONSIDERING THE EVER-EMERGENT FUNDAMENTAL FORCES WITHIN AND BETWEEN US

Strong Nuclear Force
What are the first, most fundamental parts of you? How does the energy particular to you begin to cohere into parts that matter?

Electromagnetic Force
What parts of you – what values and vulnerabilities – feel central? What parts fly around the centre in a probabilistic cloud? How do these parts interact with each other?

Weak Force

What are your satisfactions? How are your satisfactions slowly evolving into new longings?

Gravity

Where do you, your intimate relationships, and the communities you are part of have gravity? What gives you definition and density, in your relationship with others?

REFLECTION: CONSIDERING SINGULARITY

What is the longing at the core of me?

What are the emergent properties of this me, that only I can be?

What are the emergent properties of this we, that only we can be? How can a new I emerge because of us?

What is the core longing of this unique planet? of this singular universe?

892

889

893

890

894

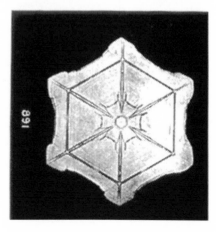

891

CHAPTER 2

ELEMENTS: COMPLEX ATTACHMENT

ELEMENTAL ATTACHMENT

I am an ill-fitting human whose early childhood was marked by trauma and neglect. Throughout life, I have struggled to find love, feel loveable, and establish places of secure belonging. As a teacher of sex and intimacy, I know all humans share this struggle to some extent.

Understanding attachment theory, and being able to identify secure and insecure attachment patterns, has been extremely helpful for me. I know that when I am – or others are – avoidant and dismissive of the importance of relationships, or anxious and preoccupied with the importance of relationships, or immobilized yet terrified in relationships, it is because of old neurological patterns triggered by deep insecurities. Personal and cultural patterns of love and belonging shape our interpersonal neurobiology. Attachment styles get grooved into the living cells and electrical and chemical signals of each person's nervous system. They show up in gender roles and social systems. Neural grooves are biophysical realities, but they are also changeable; thanks to neuroplasticity, we can learn and grow.

For relationships of mid-life, and in my teaching, attachment theory has been helpful and illuminating. It has guided me in understanding my own neural habits, and those of others, and helped me find and forge relationships that are much more secure and soul-nurturing than those I experienced in early life. But as I grow older and odder, my longings and relationships seemed to demand more complex understandings, more acceptance and self-acceptance, and new learning.

As I grow old, I find myself in love with fellow humans who are already, as I am, securely and radically independent. We don't need to foster and cherish even more independence; we are already there and we already do. Meanwhile, we are living the paradoxical truth of growing old in increasing dependence on one another. We are evermore fragile and vulnerable. However we fight and want to hide it, growing old means that loving relationships are more and more necessary and less and less accessible.

To learn to grow old in love together, I playfully imagine that we hold each other with elemental attachment patterns – those of earth, water, fire, and air. The elements offer models for intimacy that can guide human relationships. They embody complex attachment patterns, through which we can better honour our growing dependence on one another. Earth can be seen as having an avoidant – or spacious – attachment style. Water is anxious, or focused. Fire is disorganized, or transformative. Air offers secure – or delighted – attachment. The elements and their characteristic attachment styles emerge and diverge as they grow old in love together, as the planet ages.

EARTH: SPACIOUS ATTACHMENT

On the surface, earth offers relationship in the way of open hand, impassive heart, and non-reactive face. Compared with water, air and fire, we could call earth's attachment style "avoidant." But as we come to know earth's energy more deeply, we can feel in our bones how its very mass and density create a holding and enfolding that shapes us. Gravity will never let us go. Astronauts who spend time away from the hug of earth's gravity lose bone strength and muscle mass drastically, within a few days. Just being in the gravitational hold of earth creates friction and charge that shape the mass and density of all our cells. We come into being as we strengthen ourselves by moving despite this contradiction to our verticality. Within minutes of death, blood starts to pool in body parts that are closest to earth. Until then, hearts pump, and circulatory systems function electromagnetically to keep energy flowing through our singular selves. Gravity is an ongoing relationship between each one of us and the planet. We are comprised in an ever-unfolding dialectic of vertical and horizontal, movement and stasis, until death brings us closer together. The energy of aliveness is continually emerging in resistance to gravity.

Earth also holds and enfolds us in a very particular form of levity. There is a geomagnetic field generated deep inside the planet that extends for 40,000 miles outside it. The earth's magnetic field is formed by ever-shifting flows within the molten iron core beneath the surface of the planet. Iron, spun by earth's spin, responding to differences in temperature within and around it, generates electrical currents that create the geomagnetic field. The currents are not consistent, and yet they have a dynamic stability that means the magnetosphere protects and sustains the atmosphere, repelling harmful solar winds. While protecting from harm, magnetism dances with light and power. It guides all of being into alignment. Iron exists throughout every body. Ferritin is an intracellular protein that stores iron. It is produced by almost all living organisms, including archaea, bacteria, algae, complex plants, and animals, using genes that are conserved between species. For red-blooded animals, iron is the heme in hemoglobin. Magnetite, the most magnetic of Earth's naturally-occurring minerals, is found throughout the human brain, especially in the cerebellum and brainstem. Tuning into our cells, we can feel the dance of the geomagnetic field inside us while we feel its protection around us. Feeling and following our inner impulses – our somatic Yes, No, and Maybe – we can orient to earth's magnetic field, align with the planet, and find our way home.

And that ever-so stable earth beneath our feet can offer radical surprises. Earth's magnetic poles switch directions every half million years, so that what we know as the high arctic region today will eventually become the south magnetic pole. According to the record of magnetic field direction preserved in magnetized minerals in layers of sediments turned to stone, we're due for a pole reversal sometime soon.

Learning new attachment patterns from planet earth, I can learn to feel my love, and longing for love, in ways that are as spacious as they are certain. And perhaps as I grow old and desiccate, I have increased biophysical attunement to earth's form of attachment: a holding and enfolding that is older than life.

Protecting, respecting and connecting life and non-life,
without preferring,
earth's spacious attachment style
offers both gravity and levity.

WATER: FOCUSED ATTACHMENT

Water is cohesive and adhesive. It tirelessly dissolves and integrates differences.

Inside, around, beneath and above us, forever following and finding us, infiltrating and absorbing, water has what could be described as an "anxious" attachment style. Eschewing the pejorative, I call it focused. Water is so certain of its weight, and its relentless unwillingness to disconnect, that it flows around and dissolves every obstacle, following its focused attachment to the sea. Water is so deeply bonded and cohesive in its structure, its surface tension carries it up through every constriction, even plants and springs. Water molecules know how to cling. Water is so adhesive that it dissolves and integrates everything it meets, no matter how toxic or life-affirming. Water is so attached to equilibrium that it is continually morphing and moving between states to find it. The willingness and wantingness of water generates change in every enclosed system.

We are born in the partial differentiation of our cells and our selves from water. Our DNA twists and turns to hide it, but water thinks it knows better. It makes itself necessary. Water flows through us, comprising us, making up the cytoplasm of our cells, giving us thirst, taking us out if we dare to disconnect. If we learn how to love from this element that predates and incubates all life, even as it dissolves and exceeds life, we will learn to flow in the certainty of connection.

As we move around and above every conflict
while we consist of and in every solution,
we become more and more like water.

If we are lucky enough to grow old, we go from babies whose bodies are 75% water to become elders whose bodies are only

50% water. We get more solid and resistant, even as we become more vulnerable. Moist parts of communion between inside and outside dry up and close down. Inner waters cool as our metabolism slows.

Age pares us down to insoluble elements. We become more and more the unrepentant carbon heart of us. We are increasingly ourselves alone, the dust particle in the snowflake. And in this becoming, we increasingly embody the motive force and agony of water. Water's agitated pulse, uncanny capacities, beauty, certainty and insatiable longing, cannot, after all, take this.

FIRE: TRANSFORMATIVE ATTACHMENT

Fire is the oxygen-enriched expression of electrochemical processes. Heat emerges with an amplified vibration of molecules. Fire arises when chemical bonds in molecules are broken, reformed and rearranged. Fire transforms. Contained, fire radiates warmth and light. It makes a home, a meal, and a habitat out of a pitiless world. And fire destroys all that, in an angry instant. Raging, consuming, it brings our homes and our bones to dust. One moment, fire is attractive. It feels vital to securing love and community. Then in a flash, you had better run for your life. Proximity is punishment. We could call fire's attachment style "disorganized." But as we feel fire more deeply and learn its ways, we can learn to endure in the patterns of transformative attachment that flow through each one of us, and through our communities of belonging – igniting, combusting, creating.

Fire is the earth-bound, oxygen-enriched expression of a fundamental force that acts throughout the universe at all levels. As charged particles feel attraction, repulsion, and self-satisfaction, this generates both resistance (stasis) and flow (current). Resistance contains energy. Attraction moves energy. Moving energy transforms. One atom, molecule, neuron, person, and location to another, electrical currents move with a flow of electrons. All chemical actions and reactions are expressions of the transformative flow of electric charge.

Fire makes transformative leaps in the space between bodies. Friction makes fire. Touch generates life force energy; loving connection creates flow; anger and oppression create resistance. Our brains get excited, and neurons spark in ways that embody learning and longing.

In the long view, fire will die in every differentiated system that contains it. Each particularity of being is held in the long hug and relentless tug of nonbeing. All differentiated systems eventually disaggregate. Each living cell or multicellular being eventually stops. Each chaotic relationship cools. This singular universe will eventually end.

How does any thing or any system get old, given both the fundamental fact of transformative fire and the fundamental fact of its inevitable end? At every level – atoms, molecules, cells, relationships, homes, communities, societies, planet, solar system, universe – fireplaces get made. When energy is hosted in safe-enough containers, fire's transformative effects can be held and tended.

Fire uncontained
is relentless in its consumption of energy.
It combusts and destroys.
Greedily devouring its own and
others' energy, fire burns itself out.
Contained, fire's transformative
energy cooks and creates.
Fire empowers.

Fire held in safe-enough containment becomes less reactive and needy, and more stable and self-actualizing. Containment generates amplified vibration. If we learn to get old and endure in love from fire, even as our fires slow, and need more tending, we might enjoy our increasing containment. Our fire can learn to know and tend itself.

AIR: DELIGHTED ATTACHMENT

Earth, water and fire are all held in the embrace of air, the connector and collaborator who mobilizes brilliant partnerships. Air dances with all the other elements, while they play, and support each other's ongoing becoming.

> Seemingly without jealousy, anxious clinging,
> or any need to abjure connection,
> air comes in to enrich and empower
> when it's welcome and wanted;
> it goes, gladly transformed, when it's sent away.

Air maintains its own dynamic stability while offering itself to multiple creative cycles and connections. Air has a style of "delighted attachment."

Air is composed of gases, held in the embrace of gravity. Gas is by definition a substance in a state that will expand to find and fill a whole container. Gas has no fixed shape (unlike a solid) and no fixed volume (unlike a liquid). Gas is free. Air can feel and follow its own attractions, and explore others' invitations with curiosity, knowing its own free spirit will endure without disappearing in relationship. Enjoying partnership with earth, air offers its weight and soft caress to the planet and all its denizens.

LIFE FROM AIR; AIR FROM LIFE

The composition of air, which is so magically supportive to breathing and non-breathing things, is actually generated in partnership with them. Earth is often described as having had three atmospheres. The first atmosphere, captured from solar nebulae, was mostly composed of hydrogen and helium. The combination of solar wind and earth's heat drove this atmosphere away. A second nitrogenous atmosphere was formed when earth released volatile gases with the moon's arrival. This time air felt welcome enough to stay. Earth had cooled enough and become self-regulating enough, so air could feel the planet's warmth without getting burned. Air could hold on, feeling simultaneously spacious enough and connected enough to enjoy itself and earth's changing together, as their partnership endured.

And when life on earth began to produce oxygen, a third atmosphere emerged. This atmosphere's composition – 78% nitrogen and 21% oxygen, plus noble gases, carbon dioxide, and water – perfectly integrates and supports the ongoing unfolding and enfolding of all earth's life and non-life. In biotic and non-biotic cycles, in the play and pleasure of earth and air's enduring partnership, more and more earth and more and more air get generated. Abundance keeps giving itself away.

Air also has a trustworthy, creative partnership with fire that emerged with the third and present atmosphere. Air found a way to maintain a consistent oxygen level of 21 percent. This is the level at which fires ignite and propagate readily. At lower levels of oxygen, fires have no way to burn. Because oxygen is so reactive, if air carried any higher level of oxygen, fires would become more frequent, widespread and incredibly destructive.

At the present level of oxygen, fire's reactivity can be contained and tended, so that it generates transformation in fireplaces large and small, at cellular levels and ecosystem levels. Oxygen combines and combusts, in every cell as it respires, and outside of cells in what we know as fire. The system has a dynamic stability that allows trust. Each of us can choose more or less oxygen, more excitement or more peace, as we tend to the quantity and quality of our own breath.

Table: The level of oxygen in the atmosphere remains remarkably stable at 20.946% volume

Oxygen Level in Air	Effect on Human Life	Effect on Environmental Fire
above 25%	Death	Fire rages
25%	Nervous system toxicity, pulmonary and ocular toxicity. Seizures, oxidative damage to cell membranes.	Greatly increased fire risk
19-23%	Optimal life	Fires can be started and controlled
16%	Fast breathing, increased heart rate, drowsiness and nausea	Fires very hard to start
6%	Death	All fire extinguished

Air has a cellular structure that graces all things with colour, created in its dance with light from the sun. A "greenhouse effect" gets generated as air holds radiation from the sun together and apart from the infrared radiation emitted from the planet's surface. Whether the sun is there or not, whether the earth is cool or hot, air mediates. It offers a trustworthy space of stable, inviting warmth, because it knows how to hold sun's fire close to earth's warmth without fusing or confusing them.

Lightning, that generates so much magic in its dance throughout the atmosphere, is itself generated by the self-regulation of air's partnership with the other elements. With commitment to enduring the friction of their differences, charged regions in air, earth and water move to equalize themselves with fire, producing lightning's charge.

Air has a partnership with water that produces and circulates the hydrosphere, transforming the atmosphere – and so we have the intricate, complex, interdependent, all-pervading and dynamically stable system through which water lives its love and longing. The willingness of air to stay in partnership with earth the second time around meant that water vapour condensed in the containment. Atmospheric carbon then could be met and held by water, and these two together could fall as rain. Water could fill the depressions on the earth's surface and form oceans, and experience the cold, heat, push and pull of earth in a more sustainable way. Water could transpire and conspire in the things of earth, then evaporate. Held and reassured by air's embrace, it could learn to fall, and fall again.

ELEMENTAL LOVERSHIP: GROWING CAPACITY FOR DEPENDENCE AND INTERDEPENDENCE

More complex attachment patterns, like those of the elements, help me navigate the complex dynamics of growing old in enduring love with those I love. For this, I need to grow my capacity for powerlessness, insecurity, abject need, and diminishing independence.

Attachment theory was developed in a therapeutic context. How we understand our relationships through attachment theory is appropriate enough for a parental or therapeutic relationship – where the job is to nurture a child or client towards resourced independence. But independence is only a starting point. The truth of adult relationships is dependence and interdependence. We need each other; relationship is not optional. The web of us is more than the sum of us; relationship is generative.

Growing our independence, inner security and sense of worthiness is the sunny side of relationship. But what if learning how to be in respectful relationship comes not just from the side that's easy to consciously want and welcome? How can we also honour the vulnerability, dependence and interdependence that is ever-unfolding, within and around us? How can we even cultivate it, in trustworthy and conscious ways? Our relational insecurity is always unique to us, as we are uniquely in each moment. And it can only be coached and coaxed and kissed into being by those who truly want and welcome it.

As lover and beloved,

I want not only my and your power within,

even as I truly want and welcome that.

I also want more.

I want the

deeper,

hidden,

nighttime truth

of me,

of us.

I want relationship
that unfolds and enfolds
the paradox of independence and dependence.
I want lovership deep and true enough to
explore and invent
this me and you
that can only be
in the unique configuration of us.

Can there be respectful relationship that honours and invites the terrifying truth of our dependence, too? Or are we unfolding some hitherto segregated truth of craven neediness, only to be rejected, poisoned or exploited in fear-based trauma bonds? As the elements guide, caress, transform and educate my human longings, I am learning to offer love to my own and others' abject neediness. I can better honour the truth of our dependence on each other. In my intimate world, including all my relations, I want to be resourced by the attachment styles of all the elements.

EROTIC FRIENDSHIPS

What we can co-create, in intimate friendships, and counternormative communities, with guidance for complex attachment from the elements? I know the loneliness that so many feel with aging. I live alone. I am a widow. I have more precious friends on the other side of the ground than I do on this side. I want and need more time without work. I no longer convene community events and am rarely invited. Yet even with my increasing solitude, I feel wonder and joy in new forms of relationship that are flourishing in my connection with others. In a web of loving relationships where I have no function – I am not wife, partner, student, teacher – I find myself held in radical, extraordinary friendships. In the freedom of non-functionality, there are transformative possibilities. I am companioning my beloveds' souls, instead of being distracted by goals and roles. I get to keep on becoming the singularity I am, in love with other humans centred in their own singularities.

The dominant culture would have us imagine and choreograph friendships in ways that stay safe and small. We say someone is "just a friend," as if friendship were less than lovership and partnership. What if we explore friendships without the boundaries of convention that keep them circumscribed?

"Erotic friendship" is a way to inhabit intimate relationship that thrills me. Love, joy, passion, tenderness, the exchange of fluids without the assignment of roles, pleasure without possession – this feels like a path of open-hearted love that can welcome and cherish the great holy wild we are. I don't mean that I want every friendship to include genital interactions, though I integrate erotic rituals into relationships with several friends. I do want all my friendships to be deep, abiding intimacies, where we reach for ecstasies, together, again and again.

Prohibitions on the erotic keep friends away from the core of us. Cultural inhibitions and ubiquitous traumas keep us all away from our own cores. We are inhibited from fully feeling our own lusts and longings. I want to become safe-enough, and brave-enough, in my body and relationships, to more fully inhabit my own core. I want to welcome trustworthy friends to meet me there. Can we learn to reach for ecstasies together, as we weave intimacies that thrill and inspire? That is what I mean by erotic friendship.

This whole inquiry into attachment patterns emerged in an erotic friendship I share with Tricia Bowler and Michael Haines. In their teachings on social permaculture, and in our intimate life, they guide that "There is nothing to be fixed, but there is always something to be held." In workshops they offer through their "Being Held" programs, and in our lovership, they keep reminding me that when we bring "fixing" energy to ourselves and others, we undermine trust and self-trust. We fail to honour how different parts of ourselves function to enrich, guide, companion, and act as gatekeepers. When we can hold, honour, acknowledge and bring safe and wanted touch to our most troublesome or hidden aspects, we often find that supposed weaknesses are the source of superpowers. Difficult feelings don't need to be fixed or ignored; they can be held and deepened until they yield their medicine. Together we came to see how attachment theory, with its pejorative words for insecure attachment styles, pathologizes aspects of how we live and love. We could see how security and belonging are so often won through spiritual bypass, or conformity to cultural norms. We are better supported by the complex attachment styles of the elements.

My whole inquiry into learning how to get old began in conversation with a precious erotic friend, Doug Wahlsten. A decade ago, we formed a neighbourly alliance to soothe the challenges of singleness. After many years of trustworthy connection, simple suppers, erotic massages, adventures in nature, shared griefs, the dimensions of our friendship are still unfolding. We keep finding new comforts and joys. Even when we fail to conform to each other's expectations or meet each other's needs, there is a different kind of pleasure, power and dignity in moving apart from each other, while maintaining caring connection.

Doug and I come from very different social and professional worlds. We have very different experiences of gender, sexual orientation, class, family and social status. He worked as an esteemed scientist; I was a notorious sex worker. He passed as a cisgendered, straight man; I was a visible lesbian and genderqueer activist. Yes, our differences sometimes clash and inhibit intimacy. But we have both lived long lives of challenging cultural norms. Through decades of work in genetics and neuroscience, Doug contested the racism, classism, sexism, heteronormativity, and ugly prejudice that so often shape science in these fields. In my own work as a practitioner and teacher of sacred intimacy, I pushed back against the hateful messages and harmful power dynamics of the dominant culture. In very different ways, we have both contributed to weaving counternormative culture that is informed by the neurobiology of trauma, the complexity of gender and sexual orientation, the acknowledgement of human diversity, and the many nuances of empowering embodied choice and voice. Our counternormative values inform our intimate sphere; they resource our loving connection, as we bridge our differences.

Perhaps it is precisely because we find no names or models for our particular intimacy in the everyday social world around us, that we can keep on inventing a singular erotic friendship of our very own. And we both feel held in a quality of relationship we have longed for all our lives. How can we keep on cherishing each other's uniqueness, and go on evolving our friendship, while growing old in love together? We don't find guidance or models in the human world around us. But with my passion for intimacy, and his passion for science, we find helpful models for erotic friendship in the entanglements of trees, and the loves and learnings of quarks, atoms and stars.

In the erotic friendships of my old age, I experience a quality of ecstatic belonging. We delight in each other, and the delighted quality of our connection keeps on emerging. Without roles and goals from the external culture to shape our intimacies, there is no place for expectations and entitlements to adhere to us. There is no room for base-level fear, or soul-killing criticism. Every time we share a vulnerability or fear, there can be more kindness. We are able to accept what we don't like about each other, without feeling called upon to fix or change it. We co-create projects and adventures that amplify our friendship. We share ecstasies in ways that accommodate our age-related frailties and honour our age-related superpowers. I have never before experienced intimacies like the erotic friendships of my old age, and I don't find guidance for them in the human culture I inherit. But I find resonance when I look at the complex attachment patterns of the elements.

Learning about love from earth, water, fire and air, instead of just being guided by my all-too-human longings, I feel resourced by the biosphere of belonging. As a human being, I cannot want my abject dependency or love my unworthiness. Yet this is my task, as I grow old: to surrender my pride and allow my increasing powerlessness. As I expand my vulnerability with courage, I feel the elements flow through me. Together with earth, water, fire and air, we conspire to co-create relationships of enduring love.

EMBODIED ELEMENTAL ATTACHMENT PRACTICE

We hold and enfold earth, air, fire and water in our cells, skins, metabolic processes, and in the electrical energy that sparkles through our neuroendocrine systems. As a practice, we can cultivate amplified awareness of each element sequentially.

Hold a different element in each hand, either in your imagination or actually. Feel each element separately, then bring them together, and experience their blend. Feel the resistance, flirt, overwhelm, merge, 'delight and despite' of relationships between different elements. Feel your body as a cauldron where the elements dance and play.

EROTIC PRACTICE: ELEMENTAL EROS

When welcoming erotic energy with mindful self-pleasure practice, or in partner play, take time to notice the swirl of earth, water, fire and air within and between you. Stand your ground, as you breathe into your pelvis. Get wet and juicy, as you encourage the fire inside you to spark and flame. Embody connections and contradictions between the different elements.

DEATH PREPARATION PRACTICE: LIFE AFTER DEATH

Feel how the molecules of earth, water, fire and air that meet in you want to form into new forms, after the end of you. What is the impossible dream of you, that wants to go on becoming, as the elements of your body transform?

REFLECTION QUESTIONS: COMPLEX ATTACHMENT

How does your complex attachment style emerge in different relationships? Do you relate more to being like earth (spacious attachment), water (focused attachment), fire (transformative attachment) or air (delighted attachment)?

In a particular intimacy, does one person embody a particular attachment style (or element)?

Is your attachment style habitual or choiceful? What are the gifts and costs of your attachment style? Does reflecting on your embodiment of all the elements offer more choice?

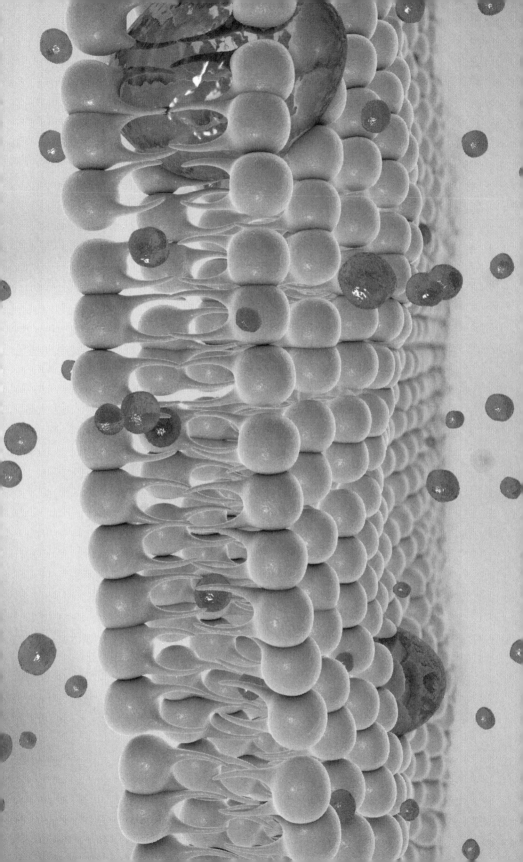

CHAPTER 3

AUTOPOESIS AND FAILURES OF LOVE

FACING THE ABSENCE OF LOVE

I feel myself aging in the embrace of exquisite, erotic friendships. But together with the increased sense of joy and rightness I feel in these relationships, I feel a corresponding increase in despair in other relationships.

Getting old means my eccentricities increasingly don't fit or harmonize with others. Some people who I thought would be my life's companions die. Others reject me. Others simply stop including me in their lives, as their own illnesses, aging, and contrary commitments increase their intolerance, and decrease the pleasures of our connection. Communities of belonging I have contributed to shaping as a leader turn out to have no capacity to hold me as an elder. Aging in the truth of loss, and letting go, means accepting feelings of emptiness and deathlike powerlessness. If I live, it is despite an agonizing absence of loving connection in places where I hoped it would flourish, and where I have tried hard to contribute to its flourishing.

I feel suddenly old, and profoundly lost, after a heartwrenching experience of relationship rupture. Just a year past the death of my life partner, I briefly explore the possibility of loving relationship with a beautiful woman. At first she seems like a kindred spirit. But quickly, our differences become the focus of unkind argument and community gossip. Finally, she banishes me from her life with a hail of invective. Even though I am grateful to be finished with the drama, my soul feels crushed by deep despair. The loss is much greater than disconnection from one particular wild, queer soul. The experience also ends, for a while, my sense of belonging to my guiding dream of queer community. Personal sadness deepens into transpersonal grief. I am overwhelmed by the scale of my incapacities, and by the world's unkindness. I thought we knew better, how to celebrate diversity and co-create community.

Just as the last wild places on earth are destroyed for profit,
Indigenous communities are smashed by global capital,
and wealth is increasingly concentrated in fewer hands,
I recognize how little I know
of how to create and co-create respectful relationships.

How do we learn to better cherish each other's uniqueness? How can we make counternormative community space that offers more than superficial, provisional belonging for our differences? We need boundaries that protect and embodied practices that connect, so we can weave resilient webs of love and justice. But we live in a culture shaped by personal and historical experiences of trauma and violence. We are often interacting with others at the level of threat management, guided by fear.

Fear wants to separate: to fight, flee, freeze, appease or dissociate. Fear wants power-over, so it can send its horrible visceral feelings of danger and distress out to less powerful beings or ways of being. Fear guides us out of connection. Love wants to connect: respect, enjoy and cherish. When love leads, we can weave ever-more trustworthy communities. We can unfold power with others, and our own power within. How do we co-create space and time where we can be safe-enough and brave-enough to choose love instead of fear?

In the embrace of the precious friendships that remain, I feel guided and empowered to go deep inside, to see if I can find a way to want to endure, and keep choosing love, despite the terrifying truth that I don't know how, and despite the soul-destroying failures of love within and around me. I find that my cells have a story to tell, and they are telling it every moment inside me.

LEARNING TO CHOOSE LOVE

Before there could be life, the molecules of life had to evolve a system to store and release energy for cellular work. Adenine triphosphate (ATP) is the energy-generation mechanism of all life. How this system came into being is earth's great mystery. The ATP system works so well, it has been conserved in every form of life, over billions of years. Each and every single-celled and multicellular being in the biosphere shares the same energy-production system. Yet each of us lives in an ongoing, embodied inquiry into the mysterious emergence and sustainability of life, in our personal relationship with ATP production. The same learning that accompanied the life's emergence goes on happening within us, with every energy demand. Each day, we have to produce our own weight in ATP to go on living. As we do so, we move through two unsustainable energy-production systems, until we find and embody a way of being that can empower an infinitely sustainable biosphere. Cultivating more conscious awareness of sequential energy-production systems, we can connect with an inner guide that can take us through terror, toxicity, shame and blame, into ecstatic belonging. With practice, we can grow patient and courageous enough to choose love.

Three different processes for creating ATP energy for ongoing life exist within us, and all three are mobilized with every energy demand.[1]

Table: Three Different Processes for Creating ATP

System	Time Required	Fuels Used	Produces	Capacity
Phosphogenic System	Immediate to 10 seconds	ATP Creatine	ATP Creatine	Buys time without net gain in ATP
Glycolitic System	10-90 seconds	Glucose	ATP Pyruvate (ferments in anaerobic environment)	2 ATP per glucose molecule
Cellular Respiration	60 seconds? (variable) to forever	Pyruvate Oxygen	ATP CO_2 Heat Water	30 ATP + 6 water molecules per glucose molecule

In the evolution of life, and every day in every 100 trillion cells of us, the Phosphagen System powers the first few seconds of self-protection and self-creation. It buys us time, without

---

1 I was guided into my whole inquiry into the sequential processes of ATP-production by Tada Hozumi, "The Selfish Activist."

actually creating new energy. Next we mobilize the Glycolytic system to take us through another burst of energy expenditure. The Glycolytic System generates ATP, but also pyruvic acid, which can shortly contribute to our fatigue and stress. But if there is breath, and time enough for oxygen to be available to our cells, a third system of ATP production gets mobilized. Cellular respiration needs the first two systems; it does not supersede them. All three processes happen with every energy demand. As we breathe deeply into our effort, reactivity, stress and distress, we move through the first two systems. If we keep going, we arrive at a place where we can mobilize and mix the ingredients of enduring love.

Short bursts of energy draw on reserves that get quickly depleted, and create waste products that are toxic to the system. When we settle into long-term, sustainable effort, we access the energy of cellular respiration. In doing so, we join in a system where our life gives as much as it takes. More life creates more energy for our own and others' lives. Cellular respiration is a much slower, more complex, time-consuming process, but it is a sweetly sustainable process. Its byproducts are not toxins, they are the stuff of life: carbon and water.

With cellular respiration, we not only know thirst; we also synthesize water. We not only feel hunger; we contribute to making food. We not only take breath; we also make breath. Living our own unique life with allegiance to this sustainable system, we participate in the ongoing self-making of an ever-emerging biosphere. Our need doesn't have to keep evoking fear. Our hunger can actually be satisfied. The longing for one more breath can be joyfully held in a larger system that wants and welcomes that longing, and needs and feeds upon that longing.

Energy required for sustained differentiation is actually created by our ongoing differentiation within the larger system.

Our longing for belonging generates
the certainty of belonging.
Both differentiation and belonging
can be born and reborn again.

Earth is referred to as the "Blue Planet" because of its abundant water. Water is made of two elements that are common throughout the universe – hydrogen and oxygen – but processes that synthesize these elements into H_2O are rare. Some tiny part of the planet's water was likely synthesized within the planet's crust, through chemical reactions at very high temperature and pressure. Some part of the planet's H_2O may have come to earth through collisions with water-rich comets, meteorites and asteroids. But once processes of energy generation through cellular respiration evolved, life synthesized water. The hydrosphere is an emergent property of living systems. Cells engaged in the process of cellular respiration are abundant springs.

We each carry within us the capacity to build cellular allegiance to this joyful system of energy generation, in which we are truly, deeply welcomed, and we belong. As we train our bodies and souls to breathe deeply, face privation with patience and courage, and find a sustainable pace for our efforts, our cells become more resourced for efficiently choosing cellular respiration. Then we can truly feel, know and grow the sustainable and sustaining pleasures of living in enduring love. We are part of a biosphere of belonging. We are wanted and needed, in all our taking and making, by an intricate self-sustaining system.

At the level of our individual human lives, the only certain way we know for postponing aging and death seems impossible and paradoxical. If we eat less and move more, we are likely to live longer, more enjoyable lives. This well-researched fact presents a living contradiction to the First Law of Thermodynamics, which states that energy cannot be created or destroyed. According to the law, there is only a limited amount of energy in the universe. If you get more, I get less. The law meets its living contradiction, as we learn to grow old in love together, and embody that learning in our living. Through cellular respiration we author, prove and embody a new law that can transform our souls and societies. Energy is created, when we breathe deeply and choose love. My living empowers your living, and your living is what sustains my living.

We co-create energy,
as we embody and experience lasting love,
when we build cellular allegiance to cellular respiration.

We can learn to enjoy our efforts and postpone our needs, while holding our fears with space enough to move through the first two ATP-production systems. These are the cellular systems that would keep us grasping for energy to sustain us from outside us, while we generate toxins within and around us. While honouring the necessity and utility of these first two systems, we can learn to develop our cellular capacity to choose love more quickly and frequently. With time, support and challenge enough, we can unfold this cellular allegiance.

By knowing the three different methods of ATP-production that go on unfolding in me, I can better feel and follow the sequences of cellular energy-production, as they are occurring. I can notice when I arrive in cellular respiration, where energy is created by energy demand. Once there, I don't need to fear immediate depletion. My energy gets amplified, as I reach for sustainable belonging in loving intimacies and joyful community. With conscious awareness of sequential processes, I become more willing and able to feel the corrosive effect of long-term, unsustainable stress. I can feel how fear and love co-exist at the molecular level, inside my skin. Resourced by awareness of molecular learning, as it unfolds every moment inside me, I can more often find patience and courage enough to choose love.

AUTOPOESIS: DEATH AS ECSTATIC THRESHOLD-CROSSING

Poesis is a Greek word that names the threshold occasion of all craft: the ecstatic moment when bits and pieces transform into a whole new thing. *Autopoesis* is a term coined by biologists Humberto Maturana and Francisco Varela to describe the astonishing self-maintaining chemistry of living cells. Capacity for ongoing autopoesis – self-maintaining, self-regulating ecstatic threshold crossing – is one that was learned by the molecules that co-create life, and it can guide us, in our lives and deaths.

The autopoesis of living systems, embodied in our cells, empowers us to stand at a threshold, again and again, unknowing. Are we here to witness the end of self, and the relational world, and all possibility of ongoing becoming? Are we here feeling fear and incapacity pull us apart? Can we stay with the goodness of all we have learned, and its not-enoughness, and open to the possibility of something new we might find inside and around us? Can we feel fear and still love fully, for long enough, and with courage, vulnerability and resource enough, to find the magic threshold-crossing *exstasis* that takes autopoesis to another level?

To evolve the infinitely sustainable energy-production system of cellular respiration, the molecules of life had to learn that sacrifices must sometimes be made. Parts of a system have to die - but they can die in a way that empowers the whole system to go on living. Willing sacrifice, for the sake of a more joyous and sustainable miracle of life, is an ancient evolutionary learning, and that same learning is ongoing, right now, inside our cells.

Our first fierce response derives immediate energy from the meat of us, without creating new energy. Our second system of empowerment – the Glycolytic System – derives energy from glucose. In order for this system to come online, there has to be cooperation of a larger community of molecules. These molecules need imagination, and communal memory enough, to sacrifice immediate wants and needs, so they can co-create energy in a way that is more complex, but more sustainable. The first stage of the Glycolitic System costs energy; it is only in the second stage that there is an energy (ATP) gain.

What remarkable learning, molecular cooperation, trust and sacrifice, it must have taken, as life emerged on earth, in order to sustain this expansion into enduring love. The Glycolitic System takes 10-15 seconds to reach its zenith, and it can be sustained at a high rate for about a minute.

The autopoetic system of ADP-ATP production learned (and goes on learning) to protect and sustain itself, and then to create a little something extra: lipids. Lipids are long chains of carbon and hydrogen molecules that have a special quality. They are both hydrophobic and hydrophilic. Amphiphile (from the Greek αμφις, amphis: both and φιλία, philia: love, friendship) is a term describing a chemical compound possessing both hydrophilic (water-loving, polar) and lipophilic (water-phobic, fat-loving, non-polar) properties. Cell walls and membranes are made of phospholipids. Our queer, amphiphilic lipid molecules create an electrochemical gradient when they aggregate. Bi-polar water molecules stop "bickering" within a lipid layer; they organize head to toe, so they can meet and match each other. Water learns to soothe and calm itself. Cell walls and membranes actually magnetize energy, because energy flows from the chaotic to the calm. In the evolution of life, this became a basis for photosynthesis, as some cells learned to harvest energy from the sun.

Photosynthesis generates ATP energy, and emits oxygen as a waste product. It was such a successful system of energy-production that cyanobacteria multiplied and transformed the atmosphere. 2.4 billion years ago, the air filled with oxygen, and the biosphere almost ended.

> *98 percent of life was extinguished in*
> *the Great Oxygen Catastrophe.*
> But even in the unthinkable terror and
> grief of all that loss, there were communities of cells
> where love was bigger than fear.

In these communities, differences could be celebrated and cultivated, while the system reached outside what it already knew, to try to go on becoming. And so it happened that a new system of autopoesis was created. The ancestors of mitochondria emerged, and then the oxygen that was killing all life on earth could be mobilized to make energy, and rebalance the biosphere. The poison was transformed into the medicine.

With photosynthesis and cellular respiration together, cellular life arrived at an infinitely sustainable system of life-giving love. Photosynthesis requires CO_2 and water; it generates oxygen and glucose. Cellular respiration requires oxygen and glucose; it generates CO_2 and water. This autopoetic system happens within every plant cell. Plants are autotrophs; their cells contain both chloroplasts and mitochondria. People and other animals are heterotrophs. Our cells contain only mitochondria. We are dependent on oxygen and glucose from plants to live, but plants thrive on the water and CO_2 we give.

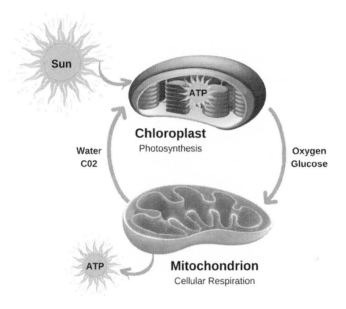

Photosynthesis and cellular respiration work together.

In the giving and receiving of love
between photosynthesis and cellular respiration,
the biosphere of life-giving love could have gone on forever
and ever.
But here we are again, facing extinction.
In climate chaos and social chaos,
there is so much terror and grief.
Can we keep bravely choosing love, and reaching for
belonging?
Can we learn to die for the sake of love?

Our most ancient cellular processes have done this before.
We know how to do this.

We can train our personal awareness of cellular processes, by engaging in embodied practices that help us move through fear while we keep choosing love. Courage-cultivating ecstatic practices are common to every ancient and indigenous culture throughout the world. They include body mortification, fasting, spiritual swimming, sweatlodges, extended lovemaking and psychedelic medicines. In time, with training, we can remember what our cells already know. We can remember:

Sacrifice has meaning, when we hold it
inside a system of reaching for more and better love.
Death can be a devotion to making more love.

FAILURES OF LOVE

Enduring love has components that we can identify, with reference to the ATP cycle going on within us. There is courageous reach into sustained, sustainable effort. Needs and failures can coax and coach – or suddenly require – our unique capacities, or our ultimate sacrifice. Love is within and between us. It is pre-cellular and cellular; it is individual and relational. It is felt and forged in enduring relationships and multigenerational communities.

Perfect love would create simple dependence on a system of energy flowing from mother / therapist / loved one /teacher/ community / biosphere in response to need. It is the experience of imperfect love, and failures of love, that guide us to find and forge independent capacities. We become love-makers as well as love-takers, as we respond creatively to failures of love. In the evolution of the energy-production systems for ATP that we hold and enfold each day within us, the interruptions and limits to energy flow are what move us into the magic of cellular respiration.

Perhaps becoming aware of the ever-emergent autopoesis we embody in the ATP cycle – the energy system we share with all of life – can help us better navigate change, challenges and failures of love in our intimacies and communities. Feeling the discrete energy-production systems that emerge as we reach for a sustainable stretch, we can learn what our cells already know about how to co-create empowerment.

With love enough,
and time enough,
we can keep finding our way
through painful failures of love.
We can keep coming back into alignment
with the deep welcome we co-create
through our cellular allegiance
to life-giving love.

EMBODIED PRACTICE: DON'T QUIT BEFORE THE MIRACLE

Choose and practice a safe activity that stretches you into a feeling of pain or privation. Examples include:

- holding an ice cube
- immersing yourself in cold water
- turning the shower to cold for 2 minutes
- exploring bold sensation

Begin the activity, and feel the scary stress and stretch. Notice your fierce first response, resisting the experiment, and choose to stay with it. (Your capacity for choice can be built through embodied practice. Track your neural learning zone.) Feel your body's panic. Notice how your mind argues for ending the practice immediately. Focus on your breath. See if you can track the moment of relative ease that comes from engaging the Glycolitic system of energy production after staying in the experiment for 10-15 seconds. Now see if you can stay with the practice for another 60-90 seconds. Quiet your breathing. Reassure your anxious mind. Look around you, noticing the world outside you. After an agonizing minute, notice the miracle. Feel relief flood your mind and body, as your cellular respiration system of energy production kicks in.

EROTIC PRACTICE: EXPLORING ENGORGEMENT

We can better understand the synthesis of energy and water across phospholipid membranes by tuning into genital engorgement. The absence of genital engorgement is not "nothing happening." Non-engorgement emerges through fascial contraction; when we are not engorged, we are actively (though unconsciously) preventing blood from flooding our erectile tissues. Explore what combination of breath, sound, movement, imagination and touch might invite release into the pelvic fascia. See if you can notice when there is an opening of one-way valves in blood vessels in erectile tissues. Notice the energy gradient you create with ease. Sometimes we can best access cellular ease and support engorgement by using exciting or even frightening thoughts, so we can focus on arousal, and release inhibitions and anxieties that generate fascial contraction. Sometimes we can best access cellular ease by simply letting go of thoughts, and allowing arousal and engorgement to unfold (as happens for many people 4-5 times each night during sleep). If engorgement is not accessible, just notice, and welcome yourself and your genitals exactly as they are.

DEATH PREPARATION PRACTICE: FALL TOWARDS FREEDOM

Fannie Lou Hamer was a civil rights movement leader, women's rights activist and community organizer who was extorted, threatened, harassed, shot at, and assaulted by racists, including the police, while trying to exercise her right to vote through the 1960's. She famously said, "If I fall, I will fall five-feet four-inches forward in the fight for freedom."

With Fannie Lou Hamer to inspire you, stretch into your full height, as you feel into your courage and dignity. Breathe deeply and connect with the biosphere you belong to. Draw on your awareness of the ATP cycle within you, shared with all life around you. Imagine yourself centred in purpose, moving toward what matters. Find a pace of sustainable effort, where you feel cellular allegiance with cellular respiration.

From this embodied place, feel how you are empowered to face mortal danger. Feel into the capacity for ecstatic threshold-crossing that is known by all your cells. Now feel into the climate chaos and mass extinction event that is currently unfolding. How can you keep reaching for life-giving love, in the face of so much imminent danger, even as you metabolize your terror and grief? How can *your* death be a fall towards freedom?

CHAPTER 4

HOLDING IRRECONCILABLE DIFFERENCES

MAKING LOVE TO OUR HABITS

A s an intimacy educator, I see how people shame themselves, and get shamed by others, for any way they don't match ideal norms. I see how aliveness is amplified, when people feel cherished *because of* their uniqueness. When our weirdness feels welcomed, then habitual ways of being can evolve in unpredictable ways, and we all get better in the blend.

> Rather than making rules for how to do it right,
> can we co-create intimacies and communities
> where our particular bodies and singular souls
> feel honoured, and encouraged to
> explore their very own, ever-emerging truths?

Arousal and orgasm often unfold according to habitual scripts that keep ecstasies accessible, but safe and small. It is the work and play of sacred intimacy to make love to our habits. What is your habitual path to orgasm? Celebrate your awesome habit! Then try making love to your habit. Let's see if I can tease your habit, just enough so it feels invited to more delight, without feeling demeaned or overwhelmed.

Try standing up for a minute, or 15 seconds, instead of just sitting in front of the computer while porn-watching. Dress your favorite fantasy in a new outfit or a different gender. Try stretching instead of clenching. Add a bit more breath, sound or movement. Notice if your trajectory towards orgasm slows too much, and your arousal gets lost. Be ready to return to your awesome habit. Try pendulating back and forth, spending a minute on your habitual path to orgasm and a half-minute trying something new. See if making your journey less habitual yields an experience that is more or less joyful. There is no correct answer, just the fun process of exploring what paths that are right for you, to access even more ecstasy.

Habitual ways of being can be honoured and celebrated for their gifts. Our habits can also have enormous costs. We can support each other in acknowledging the costs, and developing a brave longing for more, by cherishing who we are right now, while we stay curious. We can invite neuroendocrine change at the pace of trust, as we honour each person in their eccentric uniqueness.

ELEMENTAL ECCENTRICITY

All the molecular shapes of amino acids characteristic of life on Earth are "left-handed," and the sugars characteristic of life are "right-handed." This asymmetry is necessary to life. Opposite forms of both amino acids and sugars exist in the primal soup of molecules. Non-biotic chemical reactions keep yielding 50-50 mixtures of left and right-handed shapes that become inactive: differences cancel each other out. For life to unfold, molecules need to hold together in a system that encompasses asymmetrical tensions. And so I imagine that the ingredients of life had to learn the asymmetries necessary to life while held in the embrace of their elders. Earth, sun, ocean and moon must have told the molecules of life how they had learned to feel pleasure in their own and each other's eccentricities, by getting older and wiser together in the embrace of time.

As a young planet, earth was tormented by its inner heat. Eruptions of smoke and dirt kept pouring out, obscuring relationship, and hiding the planet's longing for love. Somehow, even with all the inner and outer commotion, earth managed to become brave enough to notice that its ways of trying to make itself okay were making it more and more lonely. It was scaring off the atmosphere, and blocking out the sun. Any water that landed on it had no peaceful place and time to feel held. Earth figured out that if it went on trying to soothe itself in such anxious and limited ways, it was going to wind up dead and alone. And so the planet got brave enough to hold its heat inside. It learned to feel its imperfections and eccentricities without trying to fix or hide them. And by building capacity to be with its own needs, longings and limits, without trying to immediately extinguish them, it could calm itself enough to be attractive. Earth cooled, and its inner differences aggregated into different layers. Convection currents emerged in layers of earth and generated a toroidal magnetic field that could deflect fierce solar winds, protecting the emergent atmosphere and hydrosphere.

When earth was young, it felt like it had to stand up straight and rotate around a vertical axis. But it had not been able to do that. Whether it had been born that way, or forced to change its orientation by the impact of trauma, it got off-center. Its heights and depths were all distributed eccentrically. Its axis of rotation was tilted at an angle relative to the plane of its orbit around the sun. But it learned that it could be loved and cherished precisely for this asymmetry, and it could love even better through this asymmetry. It was *because* of its eccentric tilt that the planet could offer and experience winter, autumn, summer and spring. The tilt of earth is what generates different bioregions and ever-changing seasons. If earth orbited vertically on its axis around the sun, part of the planet would always stay too cold, and part would always stay too hot. It is because of its eccentricity that earth hosts a continually shifting dance of warmer and colder, in the ongoing unfolding of different temperatures that can excite air, water, earth and sun to shape-shift, mingle and tingle, feeling multiple flows of energy through generative differences.

When earth was young, it thought it could find a steady, circular orbit around the sun. It kept trying and failing to get the distance just right, so it could stay separate and still maintain connection. But the enormous gravity of the sun kept bringing earth closer, while the momentum of earth's own energy kept it travelling forward, so it kept falling towards the sun too fast and then missing it, as it travelled through space at nearly 67,000 miles per hour, and spun around in circles at over 1000 miles per hour. When it got closer to the sun, earth's sideways momentum got even faster, and that sent it farther away. When it got too far away, its momentum slowed down, and gravity coaxed it close again. Right at the point where all could be lost, where if earth kept going it would spin out of the solar system into no more relationship, the energy of nothingness would call it back into one more round of living in love together with the sun. So much drama! But as these contradictory processes continued to unfold, through time, earth learned it could actually trust in an enduring relationship with an elliptical orbit. It could trust itself: the momentum of its own energy would keep it from disappearing into the sun. It could trust relationship: when it got far enough away, its own longing and the sun's longing would beckon a return. Instead of being guided by the fear and frustration of always getting it wrong, earth could learn to feel and follow the pleasure of an eccentric elliptical orbit in a trustworthy relationship. One focus of the ellipse was the sun. The other focus was nothing: no relationship, no orbit, no enduring in love together.

> Nothing was the place
> where fear and love always, reliably
> called earth back to love.

In finding this asymmetrical shape of enduring attachment, both earth and sun learned something they could never have learned on their own. Alone, they could only know their own longing, and that gave them no information about how to co-create sustainable relationship. It was only in connection with each other through time that they could co-create a relationship neither one could have ever imagined alone. Eccentric orbit made something far greater than a way to soothe, satisfy, or escape another's love. A double focus on staying centred in the possibility of loss and centred in enduring relationship made a system that could hang together through time. With time, the relationship could unfold even more energy, learning, and

LOVE AND DEATH IN A QUEER UNIVERSE

generative difference. Earth and sun made even-more and ever-better love.

Earth was very young when it attracted an admirer: the moon. At first, moon's arrival seemed agonizing and intolerable. The impact was massive, and earth leaned drastically into its eccentric tilt. Any more tilt would have wobbled the planet right out of the solar system. But moon set up its own elliptical orbit, and that eventually helped earth stabilize its tilt at a sustainable angle of 23.44 degrees – an angle of maximum eccentricity that could bring lasting delight to itself and the other elements. Other planets had their own relationships with earth and sun, and their own eccentric orbits, and they too pulled earth into little wiggles and wobbles with their different rhythms. Asymmetries multiplied, as the planets all encouraged each other to feel and follow the delight and despite of the wiggling, jiggling dance of attractions, and differentiations, and the ongoing, essential guidance of empty nothingness.

Ocean had its own story of aging into asymmetries. When earth and ocean both were young, the planet wanted to feel and look whole, and resist all friction. Earth kept trying to be perfectly round. There wasn't much space, in those days, for ocean to settle. Then earth got old. The planet's skin dried, and got cracked, pitted, lumpy and bumpy. Moon's arrival made a great hole where water could rest. The planet rearranged itself into mountains rising to almost 30,000 feet above sea level and ocean trenches diving 36,000 feet below. In the scars and sinks of an old and wrinkled earth. ocean had space where it could feel held and cherished. There was room for ocean to form its own sea-level sphere, and hold earth in return.

When ocean was young it tried to hide its molecular eccentricity. It kept anxiously trying to dissolve all difference within and around it. Then moon arrived, and ocean let itself feel wanted in a way that knew and grew its difference. Molecular eccentricity is what gave ocean adhesion and cohesion enough, so it could be drawn up towards moon's longing, and then return to earth, in tidal cycles. And so ocean and moon made their own rich, abiding relationship, with its own unique rhythm. Earth was frightened at first, but it soon learned it could trust the complex, eccentric rhythm of ocean's comings and goings. Earth could even get relief, by not being ocean's only, relentless focus. Earth, sun, ocean and moon could all enjoy the sweet caress of intertidal zones.

WEB OF LOVE

What a lifeless planet we'd have, if earth stood up straight, stayed spherical, and made an equidistant orbit of the sun. At many levels, asymmetry, eccentricity and imperfection create ways for energy to gather, grow and flow. When asymmetries are held together in enduring relationships, unpredictable properties of systems emerge.

I imagine the molecules of life in an emergent biosphere spent many millennia listening to the stories of earth, sun, ocean and moon. In the embrace of their elders' embodied love, they had time to learn how their own eccentricities and asymmetries could be wanted and welcomed. I imagine the molecules felt the limits, too, of what these old ones had made so far. Perhaps they even felt a frisson of indignation, at how earth, sun, ocean and moon thought they knew it all, when the molecules of life knew there could be so much more. So the molecules were coached and ignited to lean into the learning only they could bring. Feeling the necessity of their very own uniqueness nurture their energy and aliveness, nitrogen, sugar, phosphorus, oxygen and amino acids learned they didn't need to find immediate soothing in a mirror. The molecules of life could hold onto their irreconcilable differences awhile. They could hold onto each other, and let new truths emerge in loving relationships that endure through time.

As I grow old along with those I love, I feel us each become more and more eccentric, asymmetric, singular. Weaving life with other singular humans in enduring intimacies, we make a web where the whole is greater than the sum of its parts.

Because of the intimate, intricate
weave of each particular us,
I am empowered to keep
on becoming more fully me.

When we are cherished in our singularity, without being invaded or evaded, we can better burrow through traumatic acculturation, and find our way home to who and how we want to be.

In relationships where we are resourced, excited, and challenged in manageable ways, we can gradually let go of habitual numbing, dissociation, anger and appeasement – and attachments to chronic fear and pain. We can better notice our persistent fascial contractions, and open chinks in our obstinate armour. We can learn to hold irreconcilable differences within and between us. As we learn to feel ourselves more fully, we can lean even further into our uniqueness, and the co-created uniqueness of each relationship.

Becoming the one I am is a relational process. Trustworthy relationships are how I feel empowered to unfold self-trust; my capacity for loving connection grows simultaneously. Without enduring love, I get crushed – by my own habits, or by surrendering to others' expectations and entitlements. The bridges of open-hearted love we make can spiral out to touch the world around us, while they spiral in to hold us ever more intimately. I cannot be me without our love.

THE CAULDRON OF LASTING LOVE

In the experience of trauma, our integrity is simultaneously overwhelmed and undermined. The cauldron of self gets cracked. These cracks make it impossible to hold and cook the whole full feast of us. Fear and anger generate contraction, and we get stuck in constant vigilance. This can make us tough, separated, unwelcoming – without tenderness or willingness. Or the opposite can happen. The trauma of being overwhelmed generates compliance, appeasement and dissociation. We feel our aliveness as a problem we need to avoid and diminish. Belonging seems to depend on our collapse – and so we find ourselves without boundaries, passion or certainty.

I have an erotic friend who I've shared life with for more than thirty-five years. She is a fierce person, and often furious. I feel more delicate and dissociated. When we were young, my friend wanted me to be more like her, and I wanted her to be more like me, so we could stop feeling the friction of contradiction. Our differences seemed to sabotage the flow of love. But what we've found instead, by growing old in love together, is that these differences create generative tensions inside our trustworthy commitment to enduring relationship. Even now, I am still growing in capacity to ask my friend: to hold my collapse, and cherish my delicacy with tenderness. She asks me: to experience her aliveness as a call to my own aliveness, so I learn to let indignation ignite me. Together, we are living an ongoing learning of how to vibrate our love for each other into more and more resonance, and even-better love. If we hold onto our longings long enough, they keep guiding us to new delights.

Instead of meeting each other at the lowest common denominator, we are learning to lean even further into our eccentricities, and still hold on to love. With evermore differentiated and evermore integrated ways of being, we keep getting better in the blend.

We need each other's help,
to mix and cook the ingredients of us –
all the parts that feel too hard and too soft.
We need enduring relationship,
where the raw truth of us can be warmed,
slowly enough, for long enough,
until all the hard and soft,
contraction and collapse,
too much and not enough can teach each other,
instead of just contradicting each other
and cancelling each other out.

Gradually, in trust built through decades of trustworthy love, I let myself need what my friend uniquely has to give me, and I let myself offer her what I uniquely bring. We let ourselves be humbled by our failures of love, and led by our longing for even more love, until we can learn to love one another even better.

The culture around us has few models that teach us how to value our own and each other's eccentricity, and celebrate friction between us in trustworthy, enduring relationships. I find the stories of earth, sun, ocean and moon have better guidance for growing old in love together, by holding irreconcilable differences in enduring love.

EMBODIED PRACTICE: LEANING INTO ECCENTRICITY

Tie a rope together, using knots that can safely hold the full weight of a hefty human. Make a circle of humans around the rope circle. Before picking up the rope, invite each person to feel their verticality, then try leaning back, away from the group, as far as they can safely lean without falling. Now invite everyone to pick up the rope together, and hold it. Try leaning back again, together, feeling how much further you can lean away from each other when you stay connected.

Invite each person to take a turn coming inside the rope circle. The person in the centre can experiment with being held as they give their weight to the rope. Notice how you can lean into an eccentric angle when you are held by connected others. Notice how we are all different in our willingness and wantingness to be held. Some people might immediately try giving the group their full weight, whereas others go tentatively, or don't want to lean into the rope at all. There is no right or wrong way to do this - it's interesting and fun to just notice.

The person in the centre can be invited to say how they want to be held by the group - for example, "I want to be held in love (or calmness, excitement, gratitude, acceptance, playfulness....)."

In the role of holding the rope while others lean into it, notice if you are holding tightly, with anxiety, or if you are reluctant to hold. You can experiment with taking a break while others do the holding. Again there is no right or wrong way to do this - just notice.

EROTIC PRACTICE: MAKE LOVE TO YOUR HABIT

As another way to make love to your habit, try following your habitual path to orgasm, then set the timer for another twenty minutes. Explore some touch. Engage your arousal with breath, sound, movement and imagination, and notice any sensations, emotions or orgasms that unfold in the extra time.

DEATH PREPARATION PRACTICE: ALL, OR NOTHING?

Because earth's orbit is elliptical in shape, the distance between the earth and sun varies throughout the year. During the first week in January, earth is much closer to the sun (about 1.6 million miles closer to the sun than its average 93 million miles distance). If earth were to get any closer, it would be pulled out of orbit, and hurtle into the sun. During the first week of July, earth is much farther from the sun (1.6 million miles farther away from the sun than 93 million miles average). If it kept on getting farther away, it would disappear into cold, almost-empty space, no longer part of the solar system. Take time, during these times, to consider the choices. All, or nothing? Will you, and the planet, speed up, so as to keep moving apart from the sun, instead of merging (in January). Will you, and the planet, slow down, so as to turn and return to ongoing relationship (in July)?

REFLECTION QUESTIONS

Elliptical Orbit

Reflect on your elliptical orbit with another or others. Feel into the possibility of union. How could you eliminate all separation between you, and become indistinguishable from one another? Feel how your singularity resists extinguishment; it propels you apart. Reflect on the possibility of nothingness: what if you were to just keep going straight, on your own path, until there was no relationship at all? Notice whether feeling into the possibility of nothingness slows you down and changes your trajectory. Do you feel pulled back into connection by a longing for more time together, and more love?

Irreconcilable Differences

Reflect on irreconcilable differences between you and a beloved, or within a community. Is there a way to hold these differences together, so they can teach each other, instead of frightening each other off or cancelling each other out?

CHAPTER 5

WELCOME HOME: CARBON 14, SOIL AND SOULS

TROUBLING NORMAL

When people arrive at the studio of an intimacy educator, they are often driven by the question, "How can I become more normal?" The DSM (Diagnosic and Statistical Manual of Mental Disorders) offers an overwhelming list of sexual pathologies, ranging from Hypoactive Sexual Desire Disorder to various forms of Hypersexual Disorder. There is even a Non-Normative Paraphilic Disorder ever-ready to pathologize anyone who longs for something outside the box!

I see all our so-called pathologies as creative adaptations. They save our souls; they might also have great costs. I invite each person I work or play with into a counternormative framework, where the inquiry can gently shift to one of "How can I become more fully me?"

Standard sex therapy works towards normalization. Consider unintentional ejaculation – a common problem. Desensitizing creams, dissociative techniques, medications and exercises are focused on getting the person with the so-called problem to better approximate an ideal norm of penis-in-vagina intercourse. Two minutes of penetrative sex is considered a cure. Taking normalization out of the picture, we can focus on building capacity for expanded pleasure through body-based exercises and experiences. We can create counter-normative erotic space where ejaculation is welcomed and celebrated without signaling the end of a sexual experience, and where sexual experiences can include a wide range of physical and emotional pleasures that do not depend on having a hard penis. Ending unintended ejaculation is often a welcome effect of this approach, but the creation of counternormative understandings is its foundation.

Common presenting issues in the realm of intimacy education include painful intercourse, low desire and anorgasmia. Often a client's reach for healing and well-being is framed as a desire to normalize sexual behaviour and sexual response. But all these "dysfunctions" fall away in the counternormative framework of an erotic culture that celebrates non-penetrative options for sexual expression, solo sex, sex without the orgasm imperative, and the choice to not be sexual at all. When we don't make our bodies' choices into dysfunctions, we get space to listen, tease, please and engage in respectful dialogue.

Whether someone is healing sexual trauma, mending a couple relationship, exploring sexual identity or navigating a gender transition, we can support each person on their journey to healing and well-being with a critical framework that challenges the biases, suffocating paradigms and structural inequalities held in ideal norms. We inherit a culture that specifies an ideal norm for gender, sex, age, skin colour, body size, sexuality and relationship (and many other aspects of us). We embody the daily and lifelong challenges of any deviations from ideal norms. By looking critically at the regime of normal, and grounding our work and play in counternormative culture, we can offer people joyous and creative alternatives to normalization, including self-acceptance and the celebration of diversity. With a counternormative perspective, we can see that ideal norms do not emerge naturally. Sexual practices, identities and relationships unfold in an environment that punishes and pathologizes certain ways of being, while rewarding others. Normal is a social location that is continually produced and policed.

Contributing to counternormative culture and dwelling in counternormative community, we co-create a crucible in which we can go on becoming truer, wilder, evermore erotic versions of ourselves. When my attention is not focused on values that cluster around an average, I can better see what is rare, and find it precious. There are aspects of me and you that are unique, and no one else will do. I can be cherished, and cherish you in the almost-impossible unfolding of who we really are, outside of rules, roles, and ideal norms. There are extraordinary moments of life and death in which different elements interact in the creation of something new. That is the great holy wild I want for us. Those are the otherwise-unknowable ecstasies.

In this chapter, I draw on my roots in a counternormative culture, where each person is wanted and welcomed in their uniqueness, to I spin a story about rare and counternormative carbon atoms. It is a tall tale, about how carbon-14 atoms, with their longing, living and dying, guide our rare earth into its ongoing becoming. The story could be merely metaphorical. I figure that there is a one in a million million chance my story is true.

CARBON 14: ONE IN A MILLION MILLION

There is a puzzle science calls the Fermi Paradox, or *silentium universi* (the silence of the universe). Where is everybody? Why is earth so rare? In a universe so old and infinitely complicated, in a galaxy with billions of stars and earth-like planets, why is there no evidence of extraterrestrial life? According to the principle of mediocrity, carbon-based life should have evolved here, there and everywhere. Yet planet earth is so rare that, so far as we know, there is only one.

Perhaps we are one in a million million planets because of a rare, earth-born atom. One in a million million carbon atoms is a radioactive form of carbon, called carbon-14. Compared with other stardust, carbon-14 is young; it will never live to be as old. The atom begins up in earth's atmosphere, where cosmic rays send cascades of neutrons through the air. Sometimes a neutron penetrates a nitrogen molecule at just the right angle, and settles into the atomic nucleus. A newly-minted atom of carbon-14 is born.

Carbon-14 is a radioactive, mortal form of carbon. Its extra particle of self-satisfaction makes it so. Whereas an isolated neutron is so unstable that it will decay into a proton in about ten minutes, when neutrons are held in the form of carbon-14, they can take many millennia to age and end. Carbon-14 atoms combine with oxygen to create a radioactive form of carbon dioxide that is then absorbed by plants, animals and fungi, along with ordinary carbon. We are all a little radioactive, thanks to carbon-14 (and other radioactive atoms, like phosphorus).

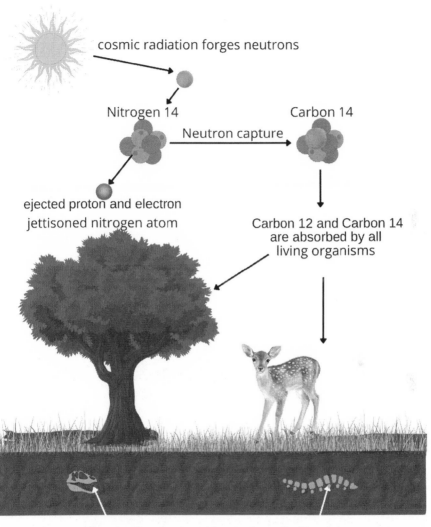

cosmic radiation forges neutrons

Nitrogen 14

Carbon 14

Neutron capture

ejected proton and electron
jettisoned nitrogen atom

Carbon 12 and Carbon 14
are absorbed by all
living organisms

after death, wood and bones lose Carbon 14
as it changes to Nitrogen 14 by beta decay

Beta decay

Carbon 14

Nitrogen 14

Carbon-14 cycle, graphic by Caffyn Jesse

Carbon-14 is rare, and yet in a world of so very, very many atoms, it is ubiquitous. (There are an estimated 7,000,000,000,000, 000,000,000,000,000 – 7 octillion – atoms in a single human body.) Everywhere there is organic life, carbon-14 is incorporated at a consistent ratio of one atom of carbon-14 to a million million (1,000,000,000,000) carbon-12 atoms.

When an organism dies, it stops absorbing carbon, including carbon-14, and its existing store decays into nitrogen. "Radioactive decay" is a bit of a misnomer. Individual atoms don't deteriorate gradually. They suddenly transform. Carbon-14 changes into nitrogen, releasing an electron and an antineutrino. Each atom is born and dies on its own timeline. A single carbon-14 atom might become nitrogen today, or stay carbon for 50,000 or more years. There is that much uncertainty. Gradual aging is an emergent property of a large group of interacting atoms. The moment of carbon-to-nitrogen transformation, that is completely unpredictable in the realm of one, becomes predictable in the realm of oh-so-many. Probabilities can be discerned, and form the basis for carbon dating. As cells containing carbon-14 atoms age, it predictably takes 5730 years until just half of the carbon-14 they integrate still exists. Surviving carbon-14 atoms slowly disappear, one by one, becoming nitrogen. The carbon-14 contained in cells stays discernable for 50,000 years, and then there is almost none.

Carbon-14 is so rare amongst its fellow carbon atoms that biological scientists assume its special properties have no impact on organisms or ecosystems. Physicists, on the other hand, imagine that each moment of radioactive decay has the power to initiate parallel universes. According to the Many-Worlds theory of quantum mechanics, each time carbon-14 becomes nitrogen, new energy is born, and worlds diverge. In the space between making no difference and initiating new universes, I dream that carbon-14 has hitherto unrecognized capacities to guide the emergence of this rare earth. If these atoms could spin their own story, it might go something like this:

Carbon 14 has an inborn longing. Every carbon-14 atom has a quantum entanglement with particles that get separated as the atom begins. As each carbon-14 atom is born, paired nitrogen atoms are disaggregated. A proton is ejected from a nitrogen nucleus. An electron gets jettisoned. Entangled particles, lost in the atom's becoming, are forever missed. And so each atom of carbon-14 wants the energy of its living and dying to serve a purpose forged in its becoming. It wants to find these particles, and welcome them home.

Carbon-14 atoms keep reaching out, in their living and dying, through billions of years of carbon becoming nitrogen becoming carbon. They guide carbon and nitrogen to partner in making a biosphere of life-giving love, and ever-welcome. Each time a carbon-14 atom transforms into nitrogen, the power of its ending is mobilized into a reach for what was lost, when the atom began. Carbon-14 atoms go on releasing electrons and antineutrinos to carry their longing and looking across the universe. They go on holding permeable boundaries of secure belonging in the biosphere, so traumatized protons returning to heal their wounds will be generative, and do no harm. Over billions of years, these atoms have guided all the elements around them to cooperate and co-create a home on earth so intricate, beautiful, open-hearted and full of longing, there is endless room and reason to come home.

CARE OF THE SOIL

Relationships that can be coaxed and coached by carbon-14's longings and capacities take time. Speed dating and hookups leave it lonely. New-made carbon-14 atoms float inside earth's atmosphere. Rain carries them to earth. If they land in some part of earth with enough wrinkles and pitted skin to hold them, they can live together with eroded minerals from earth's surface, mix with dead things, and become soil. Soil with time enough gives birth to souls. DNA, the part of any living thing where there is no exchange of carbon after cell division, gives carbon-14 a stable home to get old and die in.

When soil gets stirred a lot, it is not a welcoming place for souls. After major disturbances, soil is dominated by carbon loss for the first fifty-three years. Once older than fifty-three years, carbon sequestration becomes the dominant process. Carbon-14 held in place-based community takes 5,370 years to get through its reckless youth, as half of its life-energy is expended in a hurry. For the next 44,630 years, there is a gradual slowing down. In some quiet places on the earth, there is soil that settles long enough to hold many generations of carbon-14, including the reckless young of under 5,370 and the exhausted near-inert of 50,000. When all the carbon-14 in a soil is aging and dying at different times, and turning into nitrogen that remembers it once was carbon, and carbon that remembers it once was nitrogen, then there is a soil rich and deep with ancestors. It can generate a profusion of souls.

A deep and complex soil in central Africa, some 200,000 years ago, gave birth to anatomically modern humans. Some human ancestors stayed close to home, while others roamed across the earth. They met and mated with humanoid species that had emerged elsewhere – the Neanderthals of Europe, and the Denisovians of Asia – and made the species known as homo sapiens, aka humans. This species continues its migrations. Some humans got a chance to settle long enough to feel at home on soils that had incubated complex ecosystems. Sometimes there was grace and space enough for these humans to get old, and make sequestration places for carbon inside their bodies, and become electron donors with their being. When the soil they lived on had time enough, it could make quantum entanglements with anatomically modern humans. Then humans could emerge with DNA that included nitrogen that was once the carbon-14 of this ecosystem. Carbon-based flesh and nitrogenous DNA were related, then, with the genetic memory of an ecosystem. People and place shared a molecular language. The ancestral molecules could unfold their stories. They could coach and coax everyone around them to make a secure home, and still hold the instability of knowing that out there in the universe was something more. Carbon-based lifeforms of ecosystems could go on wanting and welcoming lost particles. They could go on reaching for them, through millennia of living and dying, while making a beautiful home to welcome their return. The soil of these places could share origin stories with anatomically modern humans. The whole placebound process had human observers then, who could tell stories of particular soils in human languages. Diverse place-based human cultures could feel and embody ancestries that reached back through specific soils, for billions of years. The many different origin stories of place-based human cultures all are true.

Other anatomically modern humans were not so lucky. Their molecules never had time and space to make quantum entanglements with soils. The nitrogen in their DNA came from the souls and soils of others. Carbon-14 held in these humans' cells didn't have direct ancestors in the nitrogenous DNA, to guide their radioactivity, and shape their processes of aging and dying. Without a place-based partnership with soil, these humans tried and tried to make belonging in the only way they knew how. Like neutrons with just ten minutes to find a stable home in an atomic nucleus, these humans found space to exist by penetrating stable systems. Without soil to guide them, their anxious longing for better belonging kept them reaching for more and more space. Over the last 5,370 years, they've grabbed up every soil in the whole biosphere. They reached out past the Milky Way into the universe. They've pushed their anxious gaze and grasping hands inside everything with mass, and mobilized more and more space inside ever-smaller particles. Rummaging through evermore intricate interiors, and ever-vaster exteriors, they kept trying to assuage their longing. Thinking they had to have more time, these humans without a soil made time expand, until their origin story reached back 13.8 billion years.

But even with all the extra space and time they kept on finding, these humans couldn't figure out how to stop, and settle, and give themselves and the world around them a little bit of all this space and time. They couldn't find space enough inside themselves to feel a settling of their inner soil. They couldn't stay still long enough to let the soil around them settle. With the hypervigilance and dissociation of the deeply traumatized, they lived in constant fear. Their fear got bigger and bigger, and it kept on making an ever-more dangerous world. Without a soil, the energy and longing of the carbon-14 atoms within and around these humans couldn't be held safe through their reckless youth. There was no quiet space and time where the nitrogen inside them could offer the learning it had gleaned through its life as carbon. Without molecular ancestors to hold and scold their fear, it got old without ripening. Their hands' anxious grasping never learned to open into a lived longing, and an ongoing offering. And so these humans' fear grew older without getting wiser. They never learned how fear that is well-loved can say its prayers, and ripen into courage; it can become fierce, focused capacity to face true dangers.

With no connection to the soil of their emergence and ongoing becoming, each of these humans was isolated and alone. Like isolated radioactive atoms, their energy was uncontained in community. They couldn't experience the emergent property of gradual aging, with all its history and mystery. For these lonely, individuated humans without a soil, death was only agony. Time seemed to be an enemy. And so they made a global economy perfectly designed to make time end.

WELCOME HOME

Like every carbon-14 atom, I am entangled with those I have loved and lost, and every path not taken. Every time I have found love, or chosen a way of life that was right for me, there has been some terrible loss. Someone felt rejected. Someone endured the agony that they, or the way of life their soul required of me, was not cherished and chosen. Every day throughout my life, I am rejected by others' choices. I live the ever-fresh agony of being unwanted. I am not right, right now, for the ongoing evolution of souls who once loved me, or evolving communities where I once was cherished. I am white, right now, and so I embody the unconscious entitlements of a contemptible culture designed to send all its agonies downstream, and make time end. There are parts of myself I despise and don't want. There are undeveloped parts of me I see in you, that I so long for.

Painful rejections and separations are often necessary. And I go on wanting and trying to weave a world in which everyone, and every part of ourselves, can be welcomed home. Can we still be wanted, mourned and missed, even as we gladly move into the divergences that are right for us? Inspired by the story of carbon-14, I dream that in our separateness, we stay entangled. We weave worlds that one day will want us home again. What if there was no person, and no part of ourselves, too shameful, ugly and unlovable to be welcomed home?

For several years, I shared monthly rituals with Tricia Bowler and Michael Haines. We took turns offering each other the experience of having a problematic part of ourselves welcomed home. We would each bring some shameful, unlovable or hard-to-hold part to be held. First there was a gentle inquiry as to its embodied presence. What is the temperature, density, colour and vibration of this part? Where is it, in your body? What words might it say, if it had a voice? We stayed curious, and kept exploring, instead of fixing. We offered an embodied welcome, asking this part how it would like to be touched. Each month, for many years, we experienced authentic, embodied welcome for parts of ourselves that have been hard to hold. Our unwanted parts came home and danced with one another.

In these rituals, parts of me that had been rejected and denied could begin to speak their truth, and show us why they existed. Though seen as problems, and parts I wanted only to hide, they often brought great gifts. I experienced celebration and welcome for parts I thought were so unlovable – even though I didn't want these parts to rule my life, even though they sometimes had harmful impacts. Over time, the embodied experience of having unlovable parts welcomed home deepened my capacity for intimacy and self-intimacy. I no longer feel I have to leave parts of myself out of awareness, or out of relationship, because they need to be hidden, fixed, or changed to make me more loveable. Having more conscious relationship and embodied love for my unlovable parts, I feel like I have more choice. I can better acknowledge unintended harmful impacts of parts, when I am not trying to hide and deny them. I can better imagine a world in which all are sacred, and no one is too lost, ugly or shameful to be welcomed home. Inspired by the story of carbon-14, and resourced by these intimate rituals, I can work to co-create a world where harm can be repaired, and all are welcome.

EMBODIED PRACTICE: WELCOME HOME RITUAL

What if there is no part of us too ugly and unlovable to be welcomed home? A Welcome Home Ritual creates space, time and loving support for welcoming and integrating a part of ourselves that feels ugly, shameful and unlovable - often a part we have tried hard to fix or change. We deepen awareness of our unwanted part, and how it exists - exploring somatic presence, and stories. We create an embodied welcome for the unwanted part - learning how it wants to be held, to move, and be seen, to be touched, cherished and celebrated. We take turns holding each other's unlovable parts, and we do this again and again.

For more information, videos and examples see the free online program at EcstaticBelonging.com, section "Belonging to Each Other."

It is important to do Welcome Home Rituals with trustworthy people. We need clear agreements that whatever we share in the ritual will remain private, and never be weaponized.

EROTIC PRACTICE: WELCOME HOME

Do a Welcome Home ritual naked, integrating requests for erotic touch wanted by your unlovable or shameful part. Explore parts of your erotic self, or core erotic theme, that feel hard to hold.

DEATH PREPARATION PRACTICE:
WHAT DO YOU WANT TO CREATE?

Imagine that, like a carbon-14 atom, your death will bring new energy into the universe. What do you do want to do with the energy that comes into existence when you die? How can you prepare for death, so your dying reaches for what you long for? Death preparation might mean writing love letters, making amends, arranging bequests, preparing papers, saying whatever you don't want left unsaid....

One of the most important gifts I have ever received came through the death preparation practice of a man I knew just a little. Huber Moore, a neurodivergent man who was a brilliant birder, was a key contributor to an art project I coordinated. Twenty years later, when he died, I received a call saying he had named me as his sole beneficiary. Even though Huber had no worldly goods to leave me, his bequest created an ongoing legacy. It has ever- after anchored me in knowing how we touch each other's souls, and how we can reach out to cherish one another with our deaths.

REFLECTION QUESTIONS

Only You

Imagine yourself as a carbon atom, playing an ordinary role in the molecules of life. Get curious as to whether you are one of the one in a million million carbon atoms that is radioactive. What makes you different from the others? What about you can only be you?

No Other Us

What are the chances that the one that is you and this particular one you love should have come together and woven intimacy? Probably less than one in a million million.... What is rare, precious and unique about your relationship? What does your relationship empower in each of you? How are you different from all the relationships around you? What is the us only you can be, together?

Soil and Soul Reflection

Are you part of a culture and community that has a deep and ancient relationship with a particular soil? Or are you like a carbon-14 atom without a soil? Is your soul individuated, so that its aging and dying is not held in the gradual aging of a community, over many millennia? Can you gain stability by connecting your soul with the soil of a particular place? If you are privileged by skin tone and colonizing culture, does connecting with the soil involve making reparations to the Indigenous people of a place?

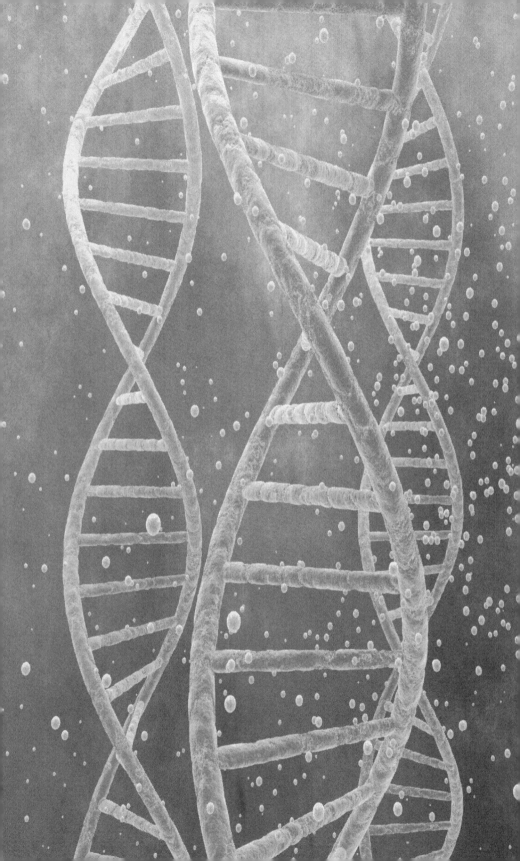

CHAPTER 6

DANCING LIKE DNA

CONTRADICTORY YEARNINGS

Some part of me stays tightly curled, all dreaming and potential. I still have juicy yearnings to unfold. Another part of me feels old and brittle. I host a vulnerable sense of being done. If I trust my body's guidance, it wants quiet days, and loving times with intimate friends. All the excitement of teaching, travelling and engaging in generative conflict feel like more than I can go on manifesting, as I contemplate what's next, and what's right for me.....

I have learned to listen to my body, and its contradictory voices, though I didn't learn very easily. As a young person, I was poor, and body needs for food and shelter felt demeaning. I was queer, and body lusts were counter-normative and dangerous. I had a uterus, in a culture without any teaching on how to hold hormonal cycles I found painful and debilitating. I experienced bullying, physical violence and sexual assaults that shaped me. My body got tight, curled in, collapsed, and constrained, and it still holds safety shapes that inhibit my full flourishing.

Now I am old, I have found my way into a life without coercions. Body needs can be welcomed and satisfied. Desires can be noticed, cultivated, celebrated and savoured. Monthly hormonal cycles ended twenty-five years ago, but endocrine cycles can go on guiding new rhythms. I am blessed with a life that resonates as just-right, and part of that just-right resonance is a committed, daily practice of challenging my body, so I can better live according to my values. Through somatic practice, I have knowledge, tools, and a loving learning community, where I can resource my commitments to joy and justice with ongoing, embodied learning. Trauma-informed somatic practice honors the ongoing impact of trauma and neglect, but not to keep us stuck in consequences. We know how to change our cardiovascular system, digestion, neurochemistry and endocrine system, as we transform fear into excitement, and capitulation into kindness. We can strengthen our bodies – while moving at the pace of trust. Honoring differences, we become more capable of holding generative tensions without collapsing or exploding. We can change habitual thoughts. We can use our wild imaginations, loving touch and daring dreams to change our DNA, with epigenetic methylation marks that can impact DNA expression in our own bodies, and potentially pass changes on to future generations.

I know I need to get wildly uncomfortable, sometimes, if I want to grow more courageous, and better live into what I want to become. Another true and important part of me, though, is done with becoming. I need an end to all the doing and new learning. I want to live into what's right for me now, and that includes more quietly being, with the biosphere, and my own intimate sphere.

What is the right balance, today, between tending vulnerable needs, and getting uncomfortable enough to support embodied change? My inquiry guides me deep into my DNA. It delights me to learn how DNA molecules fold and unfold their own embodied learning of how to age and end. They are pulled together and apart by multiple contradictions, and find purpose and passion in an ongoing dance.

THE MAGIC OF NON-FUNCTIONALITY

DNA is a molecular library of learning about how proteins can be structured and saved. Every protein is a long chain of amino acids, joined end-to-end by peptide bonds. There are just 22 different kinds of protein-creating amino acids that make up every form of biotic life. 22 doesn't sound like an overwhelming number, but since possibilities for how these amino acids can be strung together are multiplicative, not additive, potential combinations quickly become so large as to be effectively limitless. (Suppose there is a protein made of just 12 amino acids, and each one could be any of the 20 kinds specified by the genetic code, possibilities multiply into 4,096,000,000,000,000 possible combinations. If all 4,096,000,000,000,000 possibilities were present as a cell tried to make a protein, there would be – mathematically – chaos. The cell could not perform any life-giving function.)

DNA molecules came into being 3.8 billion years ago as a way to host ongoing learning. Information is held in the nitrogenous base pairs. Shapes and sequences of molecules that "fit" each other comprise a molecular memory, able to specify the exact sequences of amino acids needed to assemble different kinds of proteins. There is a mechanism, then, for living cells to repair and reproduce. Lineages of cells can diverge, while individualities go on emerging through the assortment and exchange of genes, during reproduction, through aging and epigenetic changes, and with mutations. The information that sits in a library of code is only there because of the excitement of being read and mobilized into lived meaning. DNA is a vibrating, pulsing, opening, closing system. In living cells, DNA molecules are always moving in a dance.

DNA works because it integrates useless information, nonsense and non-functionality. Non-coding parts of DNA are the places where individuality can flourish. Outside of the relentless need to matter, and to produce and reproduce matter, there is time and space to host the wild variation of each single one. Only 2 percent of the human genome is functional; it knows how to make the meat of us. Genetic variation in these protein-coding parts of the genome shows up as only about 0.001 percent. There is no measurable genetic difference between different races or ethnicities, or people with different genders, sexual orientations, abilities, or medical destinies. But in the 98% of our genome that is non-functional, there is lots of space for uniqueness to take root, and go on becoming, in all the ways that matter and don't matter. When non-coding parts of the DNA are considered, the typical difference between the genomes of individuals multiplies exponentially. We differ from one another at 4 to 5 million sites, but more than 99.9% of our differences don't affect gene function.

Non-coding parts of the DNA are places where individuation can go on emerging, through the life of an organism, as nervous system function impacts promoters, enhancers, silencers, and insulators that regulate gene expression, feeding back into nervous system function, and triggering epigenetic changes. Non-coding parts of the DNA are also places the ancestors can live, with their strange oddities silent, but still potentially available if needed.

Silenced genes can retain capacity to function for several million years, and then get reactivated into protein-coding sequences. *De novo* mutations can take hold in the non-coding genome, and hang out there purposelessly, doing nothing important. Then, when an existing system doesn't know anymore how to go on becoming, and when it can hold in the terror of not-knowing with time enough to learn, and courage enough to open, it just might be that the answer that's needed is already there, inside us. Thanks to our non-functional, non-coding DNA, we carry gifts of the ancestors, and our own individuation.

The genome of every living thing embodies respect for the magic of non-functionality. Non-functionality is space for mistakes and messiness, nonsense and missense, pleasure and play. Knowing this, it feels important to make time in my life for non-functionality. I want days devoted to having no roles or urgent goals. I want culture and community disconnected from purpose and productivity. In a world where old people have no function, and population aging is considered burdensome, the magic of non-functionality in our DNA offers guidance and support.

THE LEADING AND LAGGING STRAND INQUIRY: ONGOING ATTUNEMENT

To be, or not to be? Is a unique genome best expressed in self-replication, or in surrendering to the embrace of non-being? Is a longing for more life the poison, or is it the medicine? Each time DNA engages in the process of self-replication, it opens this vulnerable inquiry. Only one side of the double helix heads straight into the machinery of self-replication with certainty. It wants life, and can be copied directly. The other side is much less certain of what it wants and how to get there. The molecular machinery throws this side out in loops that snake around the cytoplasm. This half of our DNA is only able to go on becoming if its needs get matched in discontinuous fragments that are joined up later. Initial answers need to get refined. It gets copied one section at a time, with lots of errors, including errors that get corrected and tossed out by self/not-self guardians, and mutations that are increasingly allowed in, as we get older. This side of the double helix needs more time, and more process of being met and welcomed, corrected, and allowed to change. Is there gratitude-enough within and around for this one to want and find more life? Is there belonging enough to find another iteration of being welcomed and shared?

Our DNA engages in this death-preparation practice with every cell replication, as it separates and then integrates the parts that unequivocally want more life, and parts that are uncertain. Like our DNA, we can let our contradictory parts exist. My soul can feel self-certainty, and simultaneously engage in a vulnerable process of challenge and change. I can notice when I find myself wanted or unwanted.

I am guided by the story of DNA in my messy process of figuring out who I am, and how I can co-create the relational world I want to live in, after my retirement from teaching. Since I am no longer a paid practitioner or teacher, I am following my longing for a new kind of sacred intimacy – the kind I can only cultivate with peers and friends. I want the more vulnerable, messy intimacies unencumbered by the power dynamics, expectations and entitlements that govern client-practitioner and teacher-student relationships. I am exploring what we can co-create in communities of "equals" – even though I find the whole notion of equality suspect. Equality is an ideal that is so often wielded to ignore and punish difference. With equality as a guiding value, we are likely to suspect variety and demean inequity. We aspire to the mere tolerance of difference, instead of following the biosphere's lead, and mobilizing every difference for multiplicative ends.

Rather than pursuing a mirage of equality, I want the real, embodied joys and of ongoing attunement. I want relationships with lovers, friends and fellow-explorers that support us in becoming the ones that only we can be – with our particular, unique genetic identity. I want non-functional space and time where we don't have rules and roles, so our individualities can go on emerging, and getting mobilized into lived meanings. I want all of our wounds, gifts, powers and vulnerabilities to be able to find expression, while we keep on weaving an evermore intimate us. Living into my longing means I don't get to know how to do it. I have to go on learning, and you do too. We have to keep on finding how to come into presence with each other in ways that neither invade nor evade. It means there is a neverending, delicate process of believing, communicating, accepting and transforming our own and others' truths.

As we manifest embodied experiences of
attunement, new passions can emerge.
Ecstasy gets more ordinary, and extraordinary,
as we dance into the joys of
co-creation with erotic friends.

Relational habits and dominant cultural norms keep us falling into appeasement, accommodation and unconscious entitlement, but we can keep on calling each other in to the brave-enough, safe-enough relational space we are co-creating. Attunement is ever-emergent in the context of growing intimacy and self-intimacy. It is challenged, amplified, and sometimes lost in the sharing of ecstasies. Can I learn to stay with the generative discomfort of not having any answers, and not knowing what to do? Can I bear the vulnerability of being unwanted? As I build capacity to hold my uncomfortable aliveness, I grow in resilience and integrity simultaneously. When we do this together, our brave longing for each other can grow. We can try new adventures, be foolish and get hurt; we can disagree without diverging or constraining our aliveness.

> I can go on becoming the wild, weird one of me,
>> loving the wild, weird one of you,
>> while we evolve an evermore intimate us.

DNA – in its reliance on the magic of non-functionality, mistakes and messiness, and its ongoing inquiry into whether to be or not to be – guides me in my reach for ongoing attunement. I need to make space in which I can notice my values, tend to my vulnerabilities, and invite the ongoing unfolding and enfolding of my uniqueness. Like DNA, in its separation of the inquiries of the leading and lagging strand, I can simultaneously feel self-certainty and engage in ongoing inquiry. I can help to co-create a relational matrix where we keep on discerning the ever-emergent truth of belonging: to ourselves, to other resonant souls, and to the web of life and death – just like these brave, wise molecules of us.

EMBODIED PRACTICE: BE THE ONE

Put on some favourite music and tune into your skin. Touch yourself in a way that honours the somatic cells of you, a genetically unique being. Breathe into the one you are, and feel your breath inspire your cells. Expand into this one you are, that has never been before, and will never be again. Let your dance express your dignity.

Dance a little faster, or a little slower as you tune into your inner world. Let yourself notice how each cell carries the 99.9% of the functional genome we each share with every other human on the planet, the 75% we share with insects, the 50% we share with plants. Follow the thread of DNA into the slime molds and bacteria that are our ancestors. Let your movement or stillness emerge from your deep, inarguable belonging.

Feel yourself in time. Feel how the energy and molecules of you emerged, in the beginning of time, in the life and death of stars, and in the billions of years of learning and loving wound up into the genome of you. Feel into your own beginnings – the specific human ancestry, the trials and teachings that have shaped and resourced you. Feel into the future you are moving into. Find yourself right here, right now, centred in your skin.

Feel into your purpose. What do you value? What is your reason? What is your truth? Imagine your unique purpose, vibrating all the atoms of you. Feel your vibration dance in the DNA of you, as you join the dance of the life and death surrounding you.

EROTIC PRACTICE: FOOT BATHING

When we fall in love, we are neurochemically resourced for deep discomfort. The neurochemistry of courageous, goal-directed activity is activated. Curious, daredevil parts of us light up. We want to be wanted, and we get biophysically empowered to throw caution to the wind. Like

DNA just prior to cell division, compacting to fit six and a half feet of genetic material, duplicated, into the nucleus of a single cell, we become fiercely focused.

When we stay in love, we become neurochemically resourced for long-term bonding by finding comfort in each other. Our physiology discerns that with this one, in this relationship, I feel safer and more settled. Like DNA coaxed by proteins that provide a hydrophobic microclimate to allow transcription, we open and share.

We can commit to embodied practices that build biophysical capacities for courageous "falling in love" and contented "staying in love" simultaneously. Try a footbathing ritual. Kneel at your friend's feet, offering a warm foot bath and loving touch. Feel the feet of this singular human, in all their intricate uniqueness. Feel how much you want this person, and want to be wanted by them, in the very particular ways you do. Touch them with excitement, and passion, knowing them as precious. Fall in love.

Then, try touching in a different way. Feel all the lumps and bumps, the imperfections and ugliness of these feet, with patient equanimity, and deep acceptance. Make your footbathing into an act of service, in which you are both generous and humble. Choose love.

Like our DNA, we can hold contradictions, as we cultivate brave "fall in love" and resourced "choose love" energies, sequentially and simultaneously. We can make more and better love by dancing in the contradictions.

UNIQUE GENOME REFLECTION
FOR INDIVIDUALS, INTIMACIES AND COMMUNITIES

What is the uniqueness of you? How do you translate that information into your embodied presence and practice? What is the social environment that helps you believe in you? It's so important that you know how it can only be you, and no one else will do.

DEATH PREPARATION PRACTICE:
FOR INDIVIDUALS, INTIMACIES AND COMMUNITIES

Leading Strand: What is your self-certainty? Who are you? How do you matter?

Lagging Strand: How does the environment support and welcome you? Is it time to change and let yourself be changed? Is it time to end?

Telomere Tails: What is holding the leading strand and lagging strand together? How is this "holding it all together" function resourced?

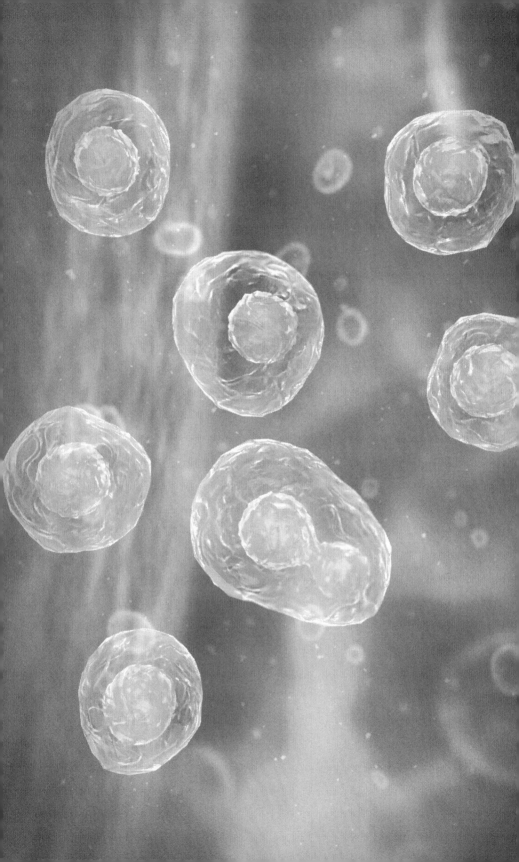

CHAPTER 7

CELLS: LEARNING IN MULTIGENERATIONAL COMMUNITY

LEARNING TO LOVE THE LETTING GO

I know that I came into this world as a unique and irreplaceable soul. I was graced with capacity and space enough to trust my soul, and keep enough pieces of it, so I could learn from the tests and traumas life presented. I could flourish in the grace, and find the kindred souls with whom I made forever bonds. My soul also found unique and irreplaceable curriculum in the field of somatic sex education. I became a writer and teacher of this soulful curriculum, and a leader in this learning community. There my most profound learning is still unfolding. It is learning how to grow old, and fail, and end. There is a living integrity to the curriculum we have co-created, that needs to be protected, nourished, held and evolved. And an essential part of that integrity is the truth of vulnerability, failures and limits.

One of my soul's forever bonds is with Corinne Diachuk. Many years ago, she came to my studio as a student who knew herself to be a teacher. She coaxed me into offering her my knowledge as if it were a professional training that could empower teaching she was already doing in the erotic realm. In the excitement of seeing my offerings ignite her, I grew into my vocation as a teacher of teachers. And through the ecstasies of ongoing emergence, with various traumas and tests, and with the delight and grace of our partnership with Dr. Liam 'captain' Snowdon, we evolved an enduring love affair that birthed the Institute for the Study of Somatic Sex Education.

The curriculum taught at the Institute gathers together many teachings, in ways that are honoured elsewhere with deep respect and financial acknowledgement. Our teachings are also the unique gifts of our three-way partnership. For a long time, in our partnership, Corinne described me as a mentor and teacher. I was attached to the role, until one day we were co-teaching an in-person intensive. Mired in some personal grief, I lost capacity to lead, and failed our students. Corinne stepped forward to take the lead from me, with power and confidence. She acted despite a fear of inciting my ire, with the insult to my dignity. Her commitment to protecting the integrity of our curriculum, and caring for our students, gave her courage. And when that night I told her of how glad I felt, and grateful, to surrender my leadership, we celebrated the crossing of a threshold into an even truer partnership. I have since witnessed a spectacular unfolding of her leadership, in the Institute and in the world far, far beyond it. I realize that my failing, and falling, and needing her help was transformational. It was my incapacity, rather than anything I had to teach, that invited her full flourishing.

I can see I had (and have still) to learn to get old, and let go, and stop being a leader. My learning has been evolving in the caring crucible of our relationship. To trust Corinne, and truly want her to supersede me, I needed years of practice. I needed to demonstrate countless failures and inadequacies, and their accrual, without having shame pull me and blame push me out of relationship. For her to evolve capacity and courage to protect our students and curriculum from my failures, she needed years of practice, demonstrating and being honoured for the gifts that she uniquely brings. Then she could trust her recognition of my failure, and her own better way and wisdom, without having blame pull her or shame push her out of relationship. Together, we had evolved a trustworthy relational space, where my letting go and her stepping up were truly, deeply generative. I could feel my failure as a falling into a deep need and longing to let go, with joyful surrender. She could take control, and feel her full power, with trust in my commitment to her and to us.

Nothing I have learned in the dominant culture has taught me to fail and fall, and surrender leadership with joy and gratitude. I see leaders busy securing power, denying failure, covering up mistakes and preserving legacy. New leadership begins by inciting contempt for what has gone before. People claim succession without humility or service; the qualification is humiliation and deposition of existing leaders. When age or inadequacies make people unimportant to the functioning of what is new and now, they are rarely cherished. But if we want to create partnerships and communities where we can be courageous, celebrate difference, learn and grow, fail and fall, age and end, and weave new worlds together, these cultural patterns are mean and demeaning. We can look to ecological patterns of succession, and our own embodied knowing, to find a better way.

With Corinne, captain, and the work and play of somatic sex education, we are finding and following a better way: the path of pleasure. We have learned how our cells can recover from the corrosive neurochemistry of distress and danger. We know to call ourselves and each other back into empowered choice and voice, and loving connection, through safe and wanted touch, breath, movement, and soul-level attunement. We have the medicine of self-regulation and co-regulation. Growing nervous system capacity through courageous learning empowers us to keep coming back home to this embodied state where we can stay connected, and learn each other. We can co-create social engagement that empowers courageous love as well as managing fear. And every time we make a choice for love, we resource ourselves, our intimates and our community to feel well-guided by pleasure, respect and self-respect. Each one experience makes it easier to make more love-based choices; we keep building capacity for choosing love, again and again. It is necessary – and it feels good – to protect our integrity, and the community's integrity, from people or patterns that could hurt and harm it. And making mistakes is a vital and valuable part of ongoing learning. Living ethics is not about getting rid of bad people. It's engagement in – and commitment to – powerful, transformative community processes.

Now there is a new learning about getting old, and relinquishing power without shame or blame, but instead, with love and pleasure. When cells are not awash with corrosive neurochemistry, or overwhelmed by injury, when they haven't lost their inherent wisdom about what's too much or not enough, they figure out how to age and end. As I feel into my ongoing learning to stop, and let go with love, and love the letting go, my cells lead and guide me.

EVOLVING TRUSTWORTHINESS IN MULTIGENERATIONAL COMMUNITY

In the narrative of Western science, cell aging and death are described as system failures. But cells live and die in multigenerational, multispecies communities. They have done so for billions of years, since life began. From the community point of view, cell aging and death can be reinterpreted as necessary learning that empowers community wellness.

For life to mature and endure in sustainable systems, we need to embody ongoing learning, as we grow old. The necessary learnings cannot be packed into a DNA suitcase. Because understanding needs to become different, at different life-stages, it needs to develop in aging cells. I playfully describe four stages of cellular life: Child, Youth, Adult and Elder.

Newborn cells need to learn to belong to themselves, and to discern what is right and wrong for them. Child cells get support from cells around them, so they can feel themselves as separate and independent. Without learning to trust themselves, cells would compromise distinctions between inside and outside. They would metabolize toxins or reject nurture. They would not be trustworthy to self.

As Youth, cells learn to belong to community, and find individuation and empowerment in a community context. Without this learning, cells would stay weak and isolated. They would not be trustworthy to self or community.

Adult cells need to learn to biophysically attune to the needs of a larger web of belonging. To allow for ongoing life within a host environment, cells need to learn to stop. With a gradual enfolding of senescence, cells won't threaten and overwhelm their host. They learn to become trustworthy to self, community, and the biosphere of belonging.

As Elders, cells need to learn to die, and disaggregate into elements that can be recycled by the larger system. Cells can unfold a process of conscious dying – called apoptosis – when ending is called for. If they don't take this path of shrinking, fragmentation and disassembly, cells perish with a loss of integrity, and a negative impact on surrounding cells. Cellular components are not readily available for ongoing life. If cells don't choose the path of conscious dying, they cannot be trustworthy to self, community, the host environment, or the web of life and death. Conscious dying is commonplace amongst our cells, and it supports whole-organism survival.

These four stages of life, and the learning intrinsic to each life stage, are fundamentally necessary to evolving sustainable existence in multigenerational, multispecies communities. Yet there is no curriculum that can be accessed outside the lived process of learning. No DNA knows just what to do; no ten commandments tell us how-to. Sequential knowings for each life stage have to be unfolded, again and again – in each cell, in every organism, and in the communities of belonging we find and co-create. It is only as we grow old and die in love together that we can embody the journey of necessary knowing. Living systems have Elders in them, doing their learning, as well as Child, Youth and Adult doing their own developmentally-appropriate learning. We are learning for each other and with each other – to embody what the whole system needs.

The difference between a traumatized cell subjected to death by necrosis and a cell that unfolds a process of conscious ending through apoptosis is a clear illustration of just what we are afraid of – that we will not to be able to mature into a choiceful and orderly end. Traumatized cells inflame to repair, but when they cannot, they die by necrosis. Cell membranes rupture, and cell contents are released into the extracellular space. Necrotic cell death has a great impact on adjacent cells, provoking further inflammation and additional cell death.

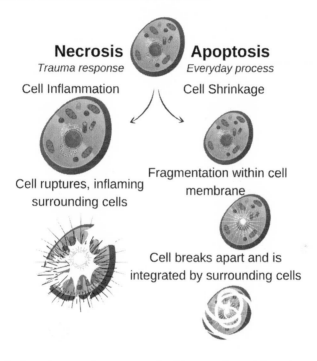

Necrosis
Trauma response
Cell Inflammation

Apoptosis
Everyday process
Cell Shrinkage

Cell ruptures, inflaming surrounding cells

Fragmentation within cell membrane

Cell breaks apart and is integrated by surrounding cells

Trauma-induced necrosis compared with conscious dying via apoptosis

I witness trauma-induced necrosis affecting cells, souls and societies. Violence and toxicity inflame our bodies and relationships. Yet I dream that in courageous communities of resistance, informed and empowered by cellular processes, we can co-create space and time for discerning better ways to age and end. Making conscious dying possible – in the face of danger, ongoing violence and systemic injustice – will take practice. We need to practice giving relational space and community cultivation to those capacities of our individual and collective nervous systems that can unfold when we are not in imminent danger: the braver, safer, and ecstatic capacities. Without embodied practice, we will stay ever-inflamed by our injuries. Only vigilance and fear seem warranted; we are in constant danger. But when we are only shaped by fear, we constantly become the very danger that we fear, to one another.

Learning to face danger without becoming dangerous is an ongoing unfolding in each cell, organism, species, ecological community and human society. What comprises danger is different, at each stage of life. Inside the molecular machinery of each single cell, inside our skins, in communities of counternormative belonging, in the biosphere, in the dance of all of being with non-being, we contain an ongoing dynamic process of learning to be discerning. Child, Youth, Adult, Elder are all engaged in developmentally-appropriate learning. Being in the ongoing learning without knowing takes courage.

As we practice courage in the face of fear, we can potentially expand into capacities for ever-more belonging, maturing into our wholeness in each stage of life, and as a multigenerational, multispecies collective. We can learn to feel fear without becoming dangerous. We can learn – as our cells learn – to choose love.

Toxins

As soon as there is life's cellular membrane, there's a need for nuanced discernment. Cells continually take in and integrate not-self elements, to support being whole and well. They continually release and refuse what would be toxic to assimilate. The pulse of taking in and letting go is the fundamental pulse of life in each cell. In - Out. Yes - No. We discern.

But what if the world of not-self around us (air, water, families, societies) contains more toxins than we can resist and release, with nuanced cellular discernments? Sometimes, we find survival by integrating toxins. We form trauma bonds. We stay connected, loving and supportive to people, environments, and ways of life that are full of hurt and harm. We find our okayness in the "Yes." Other times, we survive by rejecting toxins. Empowered by contraction and contempt, we get away, and refuse connection. We find our okayness in the "No." If there is too time to heal, we can get stuck in habitual responses. We won't be able to recognize and reject what is toxic with ever-changing, nuanced discernments, guided by lifelong learning.

We get stuck in our "Yes,"
and habitually choose love without fear.
Or we get stuck in our "No,"
and habitually choose fear without love.

Can we hold each other across generations, over time,
and make space for uncertainty?

"Maybe" feels dangerous;
so much is unknown.
But as we take time to discern the poison from the medicine,
"Maybe" is where new possibilities emerge.

What is poison as one stage of life
can be medicine at a different stage of life.
We can go on learning and discerning.

Pleasure, respect and self-respect are embodied feelings, unfolding through molecular mechanisms in our cells. Attending to intracellular and inter-cellular processes, we'll be in the inquiry, without knowing the answers. We can keep on learning throughout our lives.

EMBODIED PRACTICE:
NOTICING THE NEURAL LEARNING ZONE

Learning is impossible when we are scared and overwhelmed. It is just as impossible if we only stay safe – nervous systems atrophy. Noticing and inhabiting our personal neural learning zone is an ongoing practice. Exploring the interpersonal neural learning zone in our intimacies and communities is both challenging and joyful.

Try something new, and notice your discomfort. Feel your cells tingle. Savour the excitement. Turn to something habitual, where you know that you are safe, competent and unchallenged. Feel your cells settle. Savour the contentment. After a while spent noticing the delights of contentment, feel your cellular longing for something more. What can you do today, that will bring you into the experience of courageous, excited, developmentally-appropriate learning? Try something a little bit scary. How does fear feel in your body? Try pulling back from the edge of fear, into the uncomfortable, courageous experience of excitement. What is the safe-enough, brave-enough adventure your cells can learn in, today?

EROTIC PRACTICE: EMERGING AND ENDING

Cells learn senescence through cell divisions that segregate "stay young" and "grow old" energies. Brainstorm a list of erotic desires, separating them into "young" and "old" categories. What are the new, emerging, unexplored parts of you that want to come into being? What are the older, less lively parts of you that need patient tending, and perhaps ending? Quickly write down a list of five desires in each category. (If you only have one desire in each category, list it five times.) Then take a desire from both the emerging and ending categories, and investigate them further. Flesh them out with questions about who, what, when and how. Give your desires a timeline, and find ways to explore both emerging and ending, while staying in your personal neural learning zone.

EROTIC PRACTICE: SURPRISE ME WITH YOUR TOUCH

Many of us have experiences of unwanted touch, touch that traumatized, and touch we learned to endure. When we find touch we enjoy, we want to repeat it. But habitual pathways to pleasure can become well-worn neural grooves. If you have a safe-enough playspace with a touch partner, try growing new neural pathways by getting brave. Spend one minute, five minutes or ten minutes in an inquiry: "Surprise me with your touch." Use your words to keep the experience within your safe-enough, brave-enough neural leaning zone. Feel into scary, joyful, ambivalent or depressing memories that get ignited, knowing you are safe-enough now. Notice any extra aliveness emerging in your cells, body or relationship, with the experience of surprise. Feel what seems excessive, up to the edge of inflammation. Notice how you can consciously choose to pursue enlivenment, or let neural pathways atrophy, or spend time curiously exploring which path is preferable.

DEATH PREPARATION PRACTICE: DEATH PREPARATION PARTY

Host a death preparation party, where people can explore choosing a choiceful, helpful way of dying (apoptosis) rather than an inflamed, traumatic and traumatizing death (necrosis). What would it mean to each person present, if we could shrink, fragment, disaggregate and die in a way that supports the aliveness of those around us?

REFLECTION QUESTIONS
FOR INDIVIDUALS, INTIMACIES AND COMMUNITIES

Learning Senescence: What Needs to Stop? What Wants to Emerge?

Since our cells replicate in an ongoing inquiry of what needs to stop and what wants to emerge, can we bring the same inquiry into all we are replicating, creating and co-creating? We often struggle to replicate the same forms of life or relationship that we have had before, or that we inherit – without an ongoing inquiry into what wants to emerge, and what should stop.

Choose Apoptosis: What Needs to Die?

There are always parts of ourselves, our intimacies and our communities that are disconnected, injured, irrelevant or out-of-date. Can we create space and time to consciously reflect on what we want to let go with love, and how we can better love the letting go? Can we turn from a path of necrosis, where inflammation and rupture harms surrounding cells, to choose a path of apoptosis, where shrinkage and fragmentation support surrounding cells? Is there a part of ourselves, or a habitual way of being that we want to withdraw energy from, and disaggregate? Is there an intimacy that needs conscious uncoupling? Is there a community that has lost relevance, or become a force for harm? How might conscious dying and disaggregation reveal a truth that is hidden by overgrowth?

CHAPTER 8

MULTICELLULAR LIFE: INTEGRATING CHAOS

Conscious Chaos and Practice Dying

What we resist persists, as many have observed. We live in a culture that fiercely resists dying, as it busily manifests more and more of it. Around the world there is so much suffering and death. A global economy rooted in rationality lands us in climate chaos and social chaos, now threatening all our lives, and the whole biosphere. What we accept transforms. What if we purposefully practice dying, and spend time integrating Chaos – in its original, archetypal sense of Nothingness, the Void? In intentional times of timeless time, we can let our stories fall silent. We can savour *la petite mort* of post-orgasmic bliss. Befriending Chaos, we uncover a deep well of ongoing emergence, from which the never-before can keep coming into being.

Scientists modelling properties of matter note that patterns of great beauty and complexity emerge, when cells interact with each other in three different states: excited, excitable, and satisfied. Excited cells tickle and tease excitable cells around them, triggering transformational change. But without a refractory period, matter quickly becomes inert; all differences get neutralized. To get sustain ongoing emergence, cells need times, after a climax, when they are unexcitable; they savour being satisfied. (A refractory period can come after multiple climaxes, or one.) It is the slow savour of satisfaction, gradually opening into a willingness, and then a wantingness for more, that provides a way for molecular interactions to get complicated. Satisfaction is a foundation for ongoing emergence. When there is a reference point for our excitements, and a resting point, our desires can get courageous and go wild.

So too, when we savour satisfactions in our bodies and relationships. Neuroscientists note that neural re-wiring occurs during times we spend being satisfied. Savouring satisfactions is a practice that resources us, biophysically and emotionally, so we can better lean into our longings. If we notice our satisfactions, we'll find our way to more satisfactions, then more and more.

Life on earth was nothing but slime, for two billion years, until our ancestors figured out how to savour being satisfied. To find this kind of precious time, they needed to make cryptochromes. Cryptochromes are the molecules that track day and night, and the cycle of seasons. Once our slimy ancestors evolved these molecules, cellular life could integrate a little Chaos into its Eros. With a memory of seasons and cycles, organisms could spend time in generative rest, sweet sleep and dreams. There were times, then, to stop responding to danger, or seeking more pleasure – times to simply stop and rest. Once life knew what it was like to be satisfied, it was less afraid of death. Organisms could lean more fully into their longings, find their orgasms, and savour post-orgasmic bliss. By embracing and integrating Chaos, slime cells could dream of being stem cells, evolve capacity for meiosis, and initiate multicellular life with their collective dreams.

STEM CELLS: SAVOURING SATISFACTION

Stem cells are the first, last, and irreducible part of any multicellular organism. As multicellular beings, we evolve many parts of us, to host our contradictory longings. Root or shoot, heart or hand, brain or pelvis? Differentiate or belong? One unique genome, beginning with a single cell, generates many parts, and makes clear divisions of physical and emotional labour inside one skin. Stem cells are our basic reference point and resource, so we can grow many parts of us, while retaining the uniqueness that we started with, throughout our singular lives until we end.

To make more of us, stem cells are forever called to differentiation. To make sure there is ongoing capacity to make more of us, they need to stay the same. Forever accessible, yet always inaccessible, they are the cells that hold all potentiality inside them. They hold onto the potency of what could be, without becoming.

Stem cells' commitment to staying satisfied is not a given. It takes less energy for a stem cell to differentiate than to stay the same. Throughout the life of any multicellular organism, stem cells need resource enough to feel the call of need and longing that drives cellular differentiation, without fully surrendering to it. Some stem cells keep on heeding the call of need, while others keep choosing not to differentiate, not to have a defined function, but instead, to retain their full potency.

Stem cells in a multicellular organism are rare and precious. Skin, blood, germ or nerve cells are stuck being what they are. Stem cells need a lot of self-trust, to go on being unformed and non-functional. In protected stem-cell niches, these cells act like cherished elders, holding onto the power and vulnerability of origin by having nothing particular to do. Stress that is both safe-enough and exciting-enough evokes an opening to more. As long as we live, some stem cells are convinced to sacrifice their potency and differentiate. Just parts of the genome get expressed, in ways that depend on positionality. Roots grow down, shoots grow up, branches grow sideways, and floral meristems give rise to floral organs. Other stem cells resist differentiation and maintain their self-satisfaction. They hold a possible future in the life-giving form of not yet, not now and maybe never.

Stem-cell niches are the reference points, for each one's integrity, so a unique genome can go on knowing itself, apart from the environment it lives in, before and after the limits of whatever specific forms and relationships it can forge in the hug and tug of need and longing. Each plant or person is engaged in a continual process of holding a quiet certainty in each stem-cell niche – a self-awareness that exists apart from the pull of gravity, the lure of levity, the demands of belonging.

Stem cells contain potential. I want what I do, and who I am as I get old, to go on emerging from these cells that host the irreducible truth of me. I want time with other old people, where we have nothing to do and no one to be yet. Instead of letting who and how we are be shaped by what has come before, or by demands from the world outside us, we can support each other in tuning into these places of possibility deep within us. Can our love for each other and the biosphere go on emerging from still-unknown potencies that reside in our stem cells?

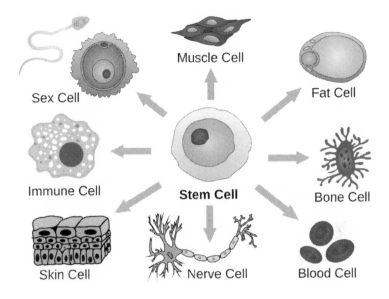

Muscle Cell

Sex Cell

Fat Cell

Immune Cell

Stem Cell

Bone Cell

Skin Cell

Nerve Cell

Blood Cell

Stem cells are able to change and transform into other types of cells found in the body. Throughout our lives, stem cells need to keep differentiating into muscle, fat, bone, blood, nerves, skin, immune cells, sex cells, and more, while also retaining pluripotency. Image adapted from Haileyfournier, Wikimedia CC

Emerging from Ancestor Slime: Radical Uniqueness

Colonies of slime mold, when deprived of heat, food or moisture, aggregate into large multicellular bodies that are more fit to survive hardship. Many single-celled amoebas gather into a multi-organism individual. Just a few slime cells in this aggregate form into spores. When these cells die, they create two new, genetically unique individuals through meiotic cell division. Meiotic cell division is not cell replication. To the contrary, it involves the death of what has been before, and the invention of something new, that has never been. A cell takes time to let chromosomal information cross over and combine in brand new ways. There is capacity for deep, qualitative change, and discernment between choices that are very different. Cell meiosis actively inhibits DNA replication, and supports the ongoing emergence of radical uniqueness. Plants, animals and fungi all populate the world with unique individuals, through meiosis, rather than trying to reproduce themselves, through mitosis. Since meiosis emerged in multi-cellular slime mats a billion years ago, planet earth has hosted the emergence of thousands of millions of unique species, all comprised of genetically unique individuals – each one of us with our very own lusts, longings and life experiences. As we live, we age into evermore radical individuation. Uniqueness is the love language of the biosphere.

It seems to me almost certain somewhere inside the 100 trillion cells of us, there is at least one totipotent stem cell that goes on maturing throughout our lives, protected by non-functionality. When it is time for our unique genome to end, then this one cell – holding the whole life-educated sum of us – could be encouraged by all our other cells to engage in an extended process of conscious dying. With that cell's meiosis, the one we are could die into a seed, a hope, a promise and a differentiation of what part of us we want to continue, and what should not. If the gamete we make happens to meet a match, then some wild interspecies intermingling could be initiated. There could be (and there certainly are) some exclamation points in evolution's punctuated equilibrium.

As I age, I can commit to embody a process of – actually or metaphorically – making one cell of me into a spore. Contemplating meiosis guides me in a process of choosing ecstatic aging and a conscious end. I want a cellular maturing of courage enough to stop replicating, and start discriminating. I want intimacies, communities and practices that support me in discerning what should go on of me, and how, and what should stop. Inspired by meiosis, I want to grow my personal capacity for generative ends.

With an eye to ancestor slime, I also feel new possibilities for collectivity emerging. Could we get slimy enough to evolve a major evolutionary transition through collective practice? A hive mind in the ancestral slime is what supports select individuals in courageous, conscious dying into meiosis. Could we cultivate "hive mind?" Ancestor slime suggests we can co-create collective consciousness, in communities where highly differentiated individuals share their daring dreams.

AGING AND DEATH AS ORGANIZERS OF LIFE

Each multicellular being is a complex system that unfolds in the contradiction between ecstasy and equilibrium. Stem cells hover in equilibrium, savouring their equanimity. Other cells reach into non-equilibrium states, as they feel and follow their longings for ecstasy. As in any complex system, when contradictory elements converge in spaces that offer a degree of freedom, and time to evolve in enduring relationship, there is a tendency to mature self-organized climax states that are barely stable. Through the life of each multicellular being, there are ongoing processes of cellular aging into climax states of self-organized criticality, unfolding along many trajectories. Whenever the stretch between ecstasy and equilibrium reaches its maximum extent, small and large orgasmic cascades are triggered with each new perturbation of an exquisitely sensitive system.

Along the way to the big avalanche ending the life of each unique genome, cell death acts as an organizer of multicellular life. Patterns of cell aging and death in developing plants and animals shape tissues and organs, and make the edges of organisms. Different types of cell death synthesize signalling molecules, guiding cellular development and DNA expression.

There are many ways our cells follow non-equilibrium paths. As one example, somatic cells replicate as they reach for relationship. A proliferation of pluripotent cells differentiates into diverse types of cells with specific functions, as each cell's relationships with cells around it evokes capacities of specific protein-coding genes within it. Disconnected cells without functional validation get pared away over time, as they choose cell death through apoptosis. We don't have a genetic blueprint guiding the production of specific tissues, organs, and networks, so much as we are formed by a cellular longing for more life, together with the integration of cell death.

By learning to dance to the ever-emerging rhythm
of reaching for ecstasy
and savouring equilibrium
we join with the web of life and death, within and around us.

We can embody more courageous reach for ecstasy,
if we stay oriented to the experience of homecoming,
and take time to savour being satisfied.

EMBODIED PRACTICE: KNOW YOURSELF

Instead of looking to reference points outside us, we can increasingly turn to reference points within us. We speak the love language of the biosphere by honouring our own uniqueness.

Interoception is a word that describes our ability to sense our internal states, and know ourselves through our own internal referencing system. Many of us live without developed interoceptive capacities. We can be completely unaware of - or very confused about - how our bodies feel, until we get suddenly overwhelmed by big emotions, or find we've skidded into a depression. Without ongoing, interoceptive self-witnessing, capacity for self-regulation is limited. If emotions need to get really big in order to be felt, we can find ourselves forever reacting to what is happening outside us, instead of choosing what's right from inside us.

Interoception is enhanced with practice in a community of practice. By staying curious, and asking each other about mood, temperature, and sensation, we support each other in growing capacity for self-witnessing. We can also support each other's interoception with our loving touch. The human skin is innervated by a network of thin, slow-conducting nerves, called C-tactile afferents, that especially respond to slow, gentle touch. C-fiber touch is known to enhance interoception. We know ourselves better when we are touched with love.

Does interoception help you land in the ever-emerging truth of you? Does it help you notice and savour tiny little orgasms?

EROTIC PRACTICE:
NOTICE AND CULTIVATE YOUR SATISFACTION

Whatever your erotic practice - with partner or partners, or alone - schedule time to savour satisfaction. At the end of any erotic activity, whether or not it results in a conventional orgasm, spend time deliberately noticing what you have experienced, and being satisfied with it.

DEATH PREPARATION PRACTICE: DEATH MEDITATION

Death meditation is a common Buddhist meditation practice. Cemetery contemplations might focus on stages of corpse decomposition, from putrescent flesh, to bones, to dust. Other ways of meditating on death might include considering death first as a dreaded murderer of life, then proof of the kinship of all life, then noticing how one dies into each moment in the experience of an endless now.

The first cell of you still exists, somewhere inside you. See if you can sense this cell, hiding somewhere amongst the 100 trillion cells of you. Now imagine that it is time for you to die. Could this one cell of you become a spore?

As a separate practice, consider a community or intimacy as an entity that was born and that will die. What seed might survive it?

Support each other's death meditation with ceremonies. As one option, people can dig their own graves and spend time in them.

REFLECTION QUESTIONS

Ecstasy and Equilibrium

How do you reach for ecstasy? Are you fully present, inside your reaching? How do you notice the outer edges of your stretch, and feel cascades into equilibrium? Are there moments when you feel satisfied, that you could choose to savour? How do you integrate peace and contentment into your being, your intimacies, and your communities?

Stem Cells

What is the one of you, that is still potential? How can you keep quiet and protected space enough for this potent one of you to go on becoming, despite all the demands and urgencies? How can you choose differently, to more carefully attend this unexpressed, nonfunctional potential of you?

CHAPTER 9

PLANTS AND FUNGI: WEB OF LOVE

GIFTS OF DEMENTIA

I am blessed to have had a life partner. We met when I was in my twenties. She died when I was almost sixty. In the delight and despite of our relationship, I found encouragement, space, reason and resource to grow my soul. As a widow still companioned by her spirit, I continue to feel and find this.

When we met, Mearnie Summers was a fiercely independent woman – a gender pioneer, community leader, athlete, dancer and lifelong teacher. She guided me into a world of lived empowerment, freedom and integrity I had not dared to dream of. I brought with me a world where queerness and gender alchemy could be celebrated with self-acceptance and pride. Together we wove a life of joy, with patches of agony.

One part of the adventure of our life together was Mearnie's journey into profound dementia. The journey took place over a decade. It was at times abrupt and shocking, and at times slow and agonizing. It was excruciatingly hard for her to let go of her powerful roles, stories and competencies. For many good reasons, Mearnie was deeply resistant to evolving conscious awareness that she needed help. This meant that at times she was bitter, resentful and paranoid. She fought hard against the need for letting go, and in the process she sometimes endangered herself and others. A big part of why she was so resistant to needing help was that there was no true help at hand; we live in a human culture where there is contempt for powerlessness. Her incapacities made her increasingly vulnerable, and her vulnerability was exploited. She offered her trust to people who stole her money. Stripped of property and roles that gave her power, she had less and less to shield her and make her welcome. She suffered agony with every small and large experience of being unwelcome, as friends and communities no longer found space where her incapacities and neediness could be gladly accommodated.

Throughout the journey of dementia, we both had to bear great grief and loneliness. We lived a lot of letting go. We also learned to feel and celebrate something that felt rare and precious. When we could come into presence together, with embodied attunement, a river of life-giving love flowed between us. We learned to love each other, and be loved, from this place. In this river of love, it feels joyful to expose need, and to tend to another's powerlessness. She could safely want help here, and help could be gladly given. Changing diapers, feeding, bathing and caring for the well-being of another are acts of love that nourish one's own lovingness.

As Mearnie lived on in the progressive unfolding of her dementia, she forgot my name. She forgot the stories of our life together. She forgot how to walk. She could no longer give words to her experience of pain. Yet even when I felt crushed by the relentless agony of losing her in all the ways I had to lose her, I also felt grateful and eager to bask in the soul-level lovingness she offered me and conjured in me. This delighted way of meeting another soul felt like home. Each day I felt – and felt her feeling – the spark of gladness we ignited in each other. The leaping heart of love was palpable, as I entered the room. We savoured our feast of delight each evening, as we sang and cuddled. When she lay dying in my arms, she said, "We are so lucky." I said, "Yes. We are so lucky." We both meant it.

The soul-level of lovingness Mearnie had to offer was not for me alone, although it was always particular and personal to each person on her care team. To meet her there, we had to support each other to bear the loneliness and grief of all the levels of letting go. We had to maintain – or at least aspire to – adequate self-care. We had to learn and practice the specific behaviours and nuanced communication patterns that supported the joyful unfolding of soul-level lovingness between us. We had to protect her from people who could not meet her in her deep vulnerability without becoming mean and demeaning. In her powerlessness, any relational demand (including a question such as "Do you remember me?") was overwhelming. Being judged as not enough (as in being contradicted or corrected) was deeply terrifying. Being left alone would often trigger deep anxiety. But with the grace of enough support, resource, goodwill and good luck, Mearnie's journey with dementia empowered her to live gladly with vulnerabilities and capacities kin to those of a plant. My love of plants and my experiences with plant medicine helped me welcome the gifts in this.

My posthumous partnership with Mearnie continues to evolve new learning, now I am on my own journey of increasing incapacity. I am letting go of roles and resources, and becoming more and more vulnerable. I need others' help. I feel the unwelcome others offer my neediness with soul-crushing agony. But I am resourced by my experience of soul-level lovingness; indeed, it has spoiled me for lesser levels of lovingness. I haven't capacity to witness, want and cherish others only at the level of their names and stories. There is something deeper, truer and forever. Plants guide, companion, coach and coax me to this homecoming.

Symbiosis

Before there could be land plants, there were lichens. When earth was nothing but bare rock, these composite organisms headed out for adventure. Lichen could settle and thrive in tiny microhabitats, where nothing else could live.

Lichen is both fungus and alga, joined in a symbiosis where two is more than one plus one. Fungi depend on sugars created by plants. Algae know how to make energy from light. Yes, differences can separate, and even trigger fear and animosity. Perhaps an absence of goodwill in crowded ponds felt inhospitable for those who preferred conspiracies of difference. Lichen got made when algae and fungi found they could mobilize the weave of their differences to empower a new way of living. Fungi could make a holding environment for just-enough water, and hold algae that could manifest energy from the sun. They could get out of the pond, then, and grow old in love together on bare rock.

Evolutionary relationships among various biological species are often conceived of as branching into ever-increasing differentiations. Lichens are a contrary convergence of branches long separated. They have evolved many times over, as different lineages of fungi formed partnerships with different lineages of algae, over hundreds of millions of years. New lichens are still forming. The word "symbiosis" was first coined to describe the relationship of algae and fungi found in lichens. Once the word was coined, the concept of symbiosis was found relevant for understanding other interspecies relationships, and eukaryogenesis. Lichens are everywhere. They drift through air. They are at home in the most extreme environments of the planet – hot, cold, wet and dry. They can survive journeys into space, and they flourish in lush forests. They grow on bare rock, and also deep inside it.

When the first lichens died, they created the first soil. Soil made space and resource enough so photosymbiont and fungus could deliciously differentiate. Plants emerged from the algal parts of lichens. Maybe the first plants were tired of giving so much of their sweetness to the fungi. Millennia of living cooperatively had incubated their wisdom, but in their integrity, they kept on longing for more. So plants headed out to find a new way of life.

BROKEN-HEARTED LOVE

The first plants on this new earth were non-vascular. To live in a world so barren, you couldn't have a heart. Yet even in a heartless world, there was this aching inquiry: what do we do with our beloved dead?

Some of the first plants found the way of hanging on. Peat moss consists of small, green, living cells (chlorophyllose cells), and large, clear, structural, dead cells (hyaline cells). The dead cells retain a huge water-holding capacity. Transport between living and dead happens by diffusion. The dead never fully decay. This allows the living to build on them. Peat moss flourishes in quiet places, where still water obstructs the flow of oxygen from the atmosphere, slowing the rate of decomposition. To stay attached to the dead in such a gentle, life-sustaining way takes space and time. Peatland ecosystems cover 3.7 million square kilometers and act as the most efficient carbon sink on the planet.

Other plants learned to have a heart, through letting their heart be broken. The ancestors of vascular plants were mosses that held onto their dead, while they simultaneously reached away from them for more life. They extended tiny roots into dead and dying, and held on, while they kept on reaching for their own becoming. Reaching into soil and sky simultaneously, their hearts stretched wide and broke open.

By tending their dying, and digging into their grief, plants learned they could increase the surface area they had available for absorption of nutrients in places where there was the nurture of decaying organic matter. Dying cells often go into autolysis (self-digestion) through the action of their own enzymes, and autolysing cells synthesize auxin. This is the hormone of finding peace with ends and limits. Synthesized from tryptophan, it is kin to the serotonin, melatonin and DMT (dimethyl-tryptamine) synthesized in animals. Auxin helped the first plants differentiate root from shoot. Roots could reach deep into peace with darkness and death, while shoots could reach into more light and life. Auxin guides roots down, and shoots up, as plants hold contradictory responses to death inside one skin.

Plant cells are perpetually pluripotent. They could function in multiple roles, yet they make decisions to differentiate. Roots dig deep into the soil, while cells in the apical meristem go on spiralling up into the light. Cambium in the trunk widens into phloem and xylem, and xylem ages into heartwood. As a tree's cells age and die, they are held together inside an increasingly craggy skin. The whole tree exists in a process of ongoing learning to use its vulnerabilities to connect differentiated parts within itself, and to connect with local ecosystems and the biosphere. As each cell, tree and ecosystem ages, there is time to learn that evermore communion empowers evermore individuation. Cellular differentiation contributes to the dignity and intricacy of a multicellular individual. Multiple multicellular individuals contribute to an ecological community. The older a tree, the more distinctive it becomes in its uniqueness. And yet it simultaneously embodies more and more connection. It is an aging tree's vulnerability, differentiation and death that invite evermore connection with insects, birds and mycorrhizal networks in forest communities. Old trees embody the cellular knowing that each one cannot live without the others' lives. As a tree grows from seedling into sapling into ancient elder, who finally fails and falls, plant cells go on maturing courageous capacity for conscious dying into expanded life.

CRAVEN NEEDINESS: BEYOND SAFETY AND SOOTHING

We need love, and sometimes, we don't get what we need. Our longings go unmet. We fail each other. In many different, agonizing ways, we lose the ones we love. Can I grow courage enough to want what I cannot have? Can I let my heart break open?

In the soil of forest ecosystems, the interspecies network of fungi, plants and microorganisms surrounds each seedling, waiting, wanting to be wanted. The web of nutrient exchange and caring communication is there, but it cannot engage with a seedling that hasn't become an energy sink. Each seedling needs to grow unmet need enough to let its heart be broken. Only then can it really open to the web of belonging. If I don't let the agony of unmet need break my heart, I will never reach for the web of love around me. I won't empty out enough to take it in.

Each individual plant recapitulates the phylogeny of vascular plants, as a circulatory system emerges in a broken, open heart. Like a tree that grows an inner conduit for water and minerals in the dead tissues of the xylem, when I reach for love with a broken heart, I have only my craven neediness to guide me. I have nothing to give; I am an energy sink. But once I connect with the web of love, I find resource and reason to grow my courage and capacity. Then I can mature into an energy source, so love can flow both ways.

Like plants,
we can learn to hold a vortex of need inside us,
as we mature bodies, intimacies, communities and cultures
that grow our courage and capacities.
We can help each other hold our unmet needs – that feel so hot,
messy, outrageous, outraged, inadequate, and agonized
– until they become a source of energy,
instead of just spreading more agony.

Like a tree in a forest,
in a biosphere of belonging,
we can grow old
inside a web of love.

Wanting what we cannot have,
we weave a web of love between
our broken, open hearts.

To actually welcome craven neediness into our moment-to-moment embodiment, we need a cauldron of trustworthy relationship. Even as we disappoint, infuriate and become irrelevant to one another, can we co-create a larger community holding of the conflict and commotion? Are there people and places we can commit to love, even when the terms of engagement need to change? When we get anchored in the web of love, we can dare to feel our agonies and grow our longings. We can honour our dependencies on one another, and the biosphere. We can stop trying to make relationship safe or small by denying dependency, or sending all our agonies downstream.

Courage matures in hearts that are called to courage by community. And communities with any longevity soon find that courage cannot be grown if fears are always prematurely soothed, and grief ameliorated. Agony needs to be endured, dangers faced, longing grown, and competency developed, even as we die inside when our hearts are broken. Truncating distress with premature soothing creates individuals, intimacies and whole societies that don't know how to get complicated and cooperative.

I am learning to hold my craven neediness in embodied awareness, as I open the chalice of my being to the delights of openly, recklessly wanting and needing love. With plants and fungi, and the web of love in forest ecosystems to guide me, I am committed to co-creating a love-based world that can accommodate unworthiness, insecurity, incapacity, and dependency.

With an embodied experience of giving and receiving love that respectfully honours both dependence and independence, there is a deeply erotic experience of empowerment and surrender. There is the ecstatic, ongoing emergence of an evermore intricate, intimate us.

EMBODIED PRACTICE: FEELING FASCIAL NETWORKS

This exercise is about orienting to the network of connection within and around us, rather than to the different objects and elements it contains.

Orient your awareness to the extracellular matrix in which the cells of your body swim. The fascial web consists of collagen, fibre proteins and a viscous fluid called the ground substance. The web surrounds, joins and penetrates every cell and organ. It is alive with signalling molecules for cell-cell communication.

Feel into your fascial network as you stretch your body. Expand into your length and breadth, feeling your bones lengthen as your muscles slide across one another. When you come to a stopping point at the outer edge of your stretch, hold it for awhile. After a minute or so of holding, you might feel a release, as fibres stretch, desiccated parts of the extracellular matrix become rehydrated, and the ground substance flows more freely.

Tune into the relational matrix of humans who support you in being you. Feel into the web, and find a courageous stretch that helps you know connection, longings and limits. Hold your stretch with awareness. After holding the stretch awhile, you might feel a sense of release, as desiccated parts of your relational matrix get rehydrated, and signalling molecules move more freely. Or you might feel discernment, as parts of the matrix differentiate from one another. There may be relationships that need to be left behind.

EROTIC PRACTICE: WANT WHAT YOU CANNOT HAVE

In habitual routines and ordinary relationships, desires stay small enough to be satisfied. We are afraid of ever feeling our unmet needs. We don't let ourselves know the agony of being unwanted.

Consider your relationship with a human intimate. Grow awareness of your longing to be fully wanted by this person. Let your awareness of your own longing grow, expand and open you, as you really want to be wanted. Notice how tuning into your wanting to be wanted impacts your energy, and physiology. Then let yourself notice and feel the grief, for all the ways you are unwanted. Let your heart break. Feel yourself die inside, as your heart is broken.

Try withdrawing any energy you have invested in stories – whether blaming the one(s) that broke your heart, or shame you feel about your choices or inadequacies. Instead, just notice your unmet needs in any particular intimacy, and let your heart be broken. Get curious about your broken-heartedness. As you die inside, can you feel new conduits opening?

DEATH PREPARATION PRACTICE: DYING INSIDE

Breathe in the oxygen generated by plants. Notice how you metabolize the nourish you need from them. Offer them the carbon that you breathe out. Feel them want the air you have so lovingly prepared for them.

Notice how you depend on the green world, want it, and want to be wanted by it. Then start to really notice all the ways you don't matter to it. There is already too much carbon in the atmosphere. You are irrelevant; you are unnoticed and unwanted. Let your heart break. Feel yourself die inside, as your heart is broken.

Be broken-hearted, and stay with the relationship. Honour your ongoing dependence on the green world. Keep wanting to be wanted by it, even in your agony for all the ways you are unwanted. Notice what happens in the tissues of your broken, open heart.

REFLECTION QUESTIONS

Symbiosis

Explore the concept of symbiosis: mutually beneficial partnerships, in which the whole is greater than the sum of the parts. Do you feel yourself engaged in symbiotic relationships with other humans? Have you interspecies symbiotic relationships? Can you imagine and/or become aware of humans forming biophysical symbiotic partnerships with the non-human world, and with each other?

Web of Love

How is the unique individuality that is you an emergent property of a web of love? How does the web of love only exist because of you?

CHAPTER 10

ANIMAL ANCESTORS: LISTENING TO DREAMS

LISTENING TO OUR WILD, WEIRD EROTIC DREAMS

The erotic imagination is unruly, rarely following cultural scripts and gender-based prescriptions about what we should want to do with whom. It conjures images that seem impossible, and unthinkable, for the sake of more arousal, passion, play and pleasure. Everyone I've ever met, through my work as a practitioner and teacher of sacred intimacy, has been beset with inchoate dreams they were afraid to dream.

Psychologist Jack Morin describes how our erotic imagination can take the most difficult material of our early life and turn it into pleasure. Old wounds become sources of arousal and invitations to ecstasy. As simplified examples: someone who has been neglected and unwanted as a child might have dreams of being infinitely desirable. Alternately, such childhood experiences might yield erotic dreams of being used without being cherished. People who have been subjected to sexual violence might have erotic dreams involving nonconsensual violence, or consensual domination and/or surrender. People who have had too much responsibility in their youth might feel chosen by fantasies and scenarios of anonymous sex in which their feelings and competencies don't matter.

Instead of just repressing fantasies that don't fit consciously held values, or intimate realities, we can choose to cultivate our erotic dreams in brave and beautiful ways. We can attend subliminal messages, poetry and metaphors in all the fantasies that show up. With more awareness, we gain more choice in how the themes of our dreams manifest in our lives. A dream of surrender, unacknowledged and unscrutinized, might pull us into relationships where we are bullied. A dream of being irresistibly desirable might leave us feeling unloved and unappreciated in ordinary human relationships. But when we consciously attend to our dreams, we can better integrate the complex (and often contradictory) longings we embody. We can weave new patterns and possibilities for our lives, guided by our dreams. My own persistent erotic dream of not mattering once used me, inasmuch as I found myself not mattering in relationships where I really wanted to matter. The same dream – acknowledged, scrutinized and mined for the deep longings it expressed – helped empower me in the personal and professional practice of sacred intimacy. As sacred intimates, we create a consensual space of "not mattering" to the realm of ordinary life, and this contributes to shaping the extra-ordinary space and time that we meet in.

When our wild, weird erotic imaginations find a welcoming soil, they can take root and grow great guiding dreams. Then lives transform. People feel empowered to jettison social expectations, inhibitions and compulsions. Again and again, I've seen magic unfurl, as radically different people, from many walks of life, in their seventies and their twenties, have found their own peculiar ways to lives of joy.

We can stop following the rules and playing the roles
that suffocate our longings,
and co-create a living ethos of true belonging.
We can come home to integrity, in intimacies resourced by
ecstasies, by listening to our dreams.

LISTENING TO CELLULAR DREAMS

As a child and a teenager, I was odd and unfitting. I was bullied and shamed, and told I did not belong. I barely survived, but in my twenties, I found resonant others. Eventually, I found and forged culture and community that supported my living as an erotic explorer, engaged in counternormative intimacies and community activism. With a sigh of relief, in my thirties, I had more time and space to dream. I could feel how my cells longed for even better, even more. I found my way to sobriety, and recovery community, which remain foundations for my life.

In my forties, I began receiving regular bodywork after an illness. Some energy channel opened, so I could better discern barriers to ecstatic life I held within me. I felt increasing awareness of a powerful, inconvenient, erotic life-force energy, wound up with inchoate cellular memories of early life trauma. Terror and desire were braided together inside my skin.

Instead of finding a way to repress or evade my awful new awareness, I was able to trust that it mattered. I listened to my cellular dreams. My cells longed for something I could not name – something I had no knowledge or experience of. The longing guided me into the world of body-based sexual healing and sacred intimacy.

I found some "sexual healing" practitioners who were truly harmful, but I kept on looking and learning, until I found other practitioners who were able to touch me in ways that coaxed and coached my healing and well-being. I opened my own practice as a sacred intimate, and developed teachings on the neurobiology of trauma and pleasure. I found I could meet clients in one-to-one sessions, body-to-body and soul-to-soul, and help them connect with their own sacred erotic life-force energy. I could bring the practices into my friendships, and we could co-create deep intimacy. Some years later, I became a teacher. I found and founded a whole community of people who could love and touch me in ways that healed and transformed. With a sigh of relief, I had time and space to dream. I could feel how my cells longed for even more.

In my fifties, I intersected with the world of sacred psychedelic medicines. Thanks to my occasional, ritual use of psychedelics including MDMA, Psilocybin, DMT, LSD, Mescaline and Ayahuasca, I experienced more embodied transformations. There is a neural learning window for social belonging that closes in late adolescence. I had a cellular feeling of not fully belonging that was cemented into me biophysically by early life experiences of trauma and neglect. With the help of these medicines, I was able to experience something deeply different. Integrating ritual experiences of medicine into my sobriety and my relational world, I found I could manifest more and more authentic belonging, in more and more resonant intimacies.

Now in my mid-sixties, I am still leaning into new longings. At the same time, I am blessed by knowing: listening to my cellular dreams has guided me home.

LISTENING TO IMAGINAL CELLS

In the history of life on earth, there is much proof of the efficacy of dreams. New beings and ways of being evolved, and we go on becoming.

600 million years ago, land-based life was just a dream of lichens on bare rock. Then plants emerged from soils made by generations of lichens living and dying. Fungi grew into mycorrhizal networks. Vascular plants got roots, and soared. Brave microscopic animals were also part of these first land-based communities; bacteria, algae, and fungi together embraced the adventure of co-evolving new ways of living and loving together on the land. Then some of the free-living microscopic beings so essential to the generative cycles of life and death got frustrated with the limits to their freedom. They dreamed of a way of life that wasn't so focused on growth and maintenance. They wanted more erotic potential, and more scope for lifelong learning. They imagined a way of living and dying together through time that could support even more differentiation and even more unity. They dreamed of life cycles and ecological niches that would give diverse parts of themselves sequential chances to flourish. They evolved a way to age into having tough exteriors, and wings. It took many millennia to figure out how to integrate metamorphosis into aging and conscious dying. The actual embodiment of metamorphosis needs to manifest through the aging and dying of each individual animal, through different developmental stages. Each organism and ecosystem needs resource and patience enough to host the whole unfolding. Given time to age, die, and be reborn, different parts of an animal's DNA could manifest very different possibilities and proteins at different life stages.

Fruit flies have been studied extensively because of their genetic similarity to humans. This is the story of a fruit fly's life. It begins in an egg, where a genetically unique zygote generates the many cells of the larva. Cells that will produce adult structures are put aside in imaginal discs. Imaginal discs begin as groups of 10–50 cells along the outside edge of the developing embryo. These cells congregate, then envaginate, making little bags of cells inside the larva that are only connected to the epidermis by a thin stalk. In their marginal spaces, imaginal cells grow into more complex discs. Though rejected as unfit to guide the growth-based economy of larval development, imaginal cells keep on dreaming, while the larval body fattens through three stages. In its last stage, the soft, fat larva starts wandering and feeding on itself. The skin of the larval body toughens and darkens as a prepupa forms.

This is a transition time, where each organism has to make its own decision. It is obvious that the growth-based stage of life has reached its limit. Will the animal continue development, and form an adult, or is it best to enter a diapause state? A decision is made, with careful evaluation of whether or not there is a possible welcome for a mature insect in the world around it. Diapause means pushing the pause button on the process of aging into what is possible. By proceeding slowly, there can be ongoing decision-making about what's next.

If the insect decides to proceed, metamorphosis begins. Imaginal discs move outside the larva body into the free space under the pupal case. The discs unfold, elongate, and fuse together into the external structures of the adult fly. This external structure holds the process as enzymes tear through each larva cell's proteins, releasing the ingredients of life into a rich molecular soup. While imaginal cells hold the external form and guide the new becoming, stem cells emerge from quiet hiding places deep inside. They mobilize the ingredients of life from the dead larva to fuel rapid cell division and differentiation.

Cells in the head unfold into a complex brain, antennae, and an expressive face with enormous eyes. Mouths become complex enough for the oral-genital pleasuring that flies enjoy. The animal develops a nervous system, heart and circulatory system, digestive system, endocrine system, breathing tubes, and complex genital structures that can be described as penetrative, receptive or gynandromorph.

INSECT EROS

Multicellular algae, and soft-bodied animals like worms, are often simultaneous hermaphrodites. They have both penetrative and receptive reproductive organs. Sex often happens in great groups. The process is so juicy that ejaculate forms a slime tube around the ecstatic bodies. Reproduction happens if sperm manage to swim through the slime tube into another worm or worms' receiving parts, where oocytes mature and new organisms are incubated.

Insects evolved inside the dream of making Eros even better. After experiencing the joys of living as a worm for several days, and going through metamorphosis, the adult fruit fly lives for several weeks. Much of adult life is spent in erotic communion with other flies. Flies nap mid-day and mid-night, and feed in the evening, but since they are no longer focused on growth, most of their days and nights can be devoted to pleasure. All the delights of adult Eros are not immediately accessible. It takes time and learning for each fly to figure out what is possible.

After emerging from the pupal case, the "newborn" adult insect is soft. It needs achingly vulnerable hours to mature the tough outer skin and functional wings of a sexually active adult. Flies learn how to have sex from watching other flies, and by listening to their own bodies. Flies with penetrative parts are sexually active within hours of emerging. Flies with receptive parts typically wait a few days. Flies are sexually active with all genders and with other fly species. Courtship involves much dancing and singing. Oral pleasures precede copulations that last around 15–20 minutes (in a life that is only a few weeks long). Flies with oocytes collect and store sperm from multiple partners, so they have many choices. Eggs are smeared with feces, so that the microorganisms with whom a mother fly shares life can welcome each newborn into its unique becoming.

When the fly dies this time, no pupa is needed to host its ongoing becoming. After so much pleasure, it has lived into the future it always imagined. Held in the larger pupal case of the biosphere of belonging, its biome is there to assist in disaggregating the elements of this one's terminal uniqueness. Death makes the elements of life available for the flourishing of more life in the larger community.

Insects evolved their beautiful lives alongside plants, through millennia of learning to celebrate each other's gifts and learn from each other's differences. Some plants wanted to live into their metamorphosis, like their insect friends. They integrated ecstatic aging and conscious dying into annual cycles. These plants made deciduous leaves that could fly, and die, and carry the elements of life far into the world around them. Flower temples hosted the maturing of the next generation, and tempted and delighted insect friends. Fruit supported the development of seeds and made a feast for insects, along with offering juice and joy to the fungus and bacteria that are so necessary to everyone's ongoing becoming. Everyone felt cherished in the ecstatic embrace of the community they were co-creating. They could witness, feel and grow into all that was possible, through living and dying together without end.

LAND ANIMALS EMERGE FROM A COLLECTIVE DREAM

With all the land-based life and death created by insects and plants, there were abundant molecules of life available to return to ponds. But all too soon, it became apparent that these gifts were overwhelming. An abundance of nitrogen and phosphorus would briefly allow a celebratory effusion of life in aquatic ecosystems. Then so much growth, and so much flourishing, meant systems of harvesting more life from death couldn't keep up.

In freshwater ponds, the effects of massive decay (eutrophication) were terrible. Whole ecosystems crashed. Ponds became toxic. Everything died. Eutrophication was also killing off coastal ocean ecosystems, as well as meadows, forests and bogs.

Piled-up dead bodies were poisoning the world. The beautiful, intricate biosphere did not have enough capacity to recycle the elements of life to support more life. It looked like the whole system of life-giving love was going to end in eutrophication. The ancestors conspired. They tried and tried to figure out a way they could all endure in love together. It was obvious they needed an entirely new form of life to mobilize the elements of life in a way that could bring more life. And so, I imagine, the beings of earth co-created vertebrates; we emerged from a collective dream.

Plants offered their diverse understandings of how to generate body shapes, and incubate embryos inside. Insects brought all their learning about ecstatic aging, and hosting imaginal cells in order to guide metamorphosis. Fungi brought capacities to break down dead organic matter with extracellular digestion, so stardust could be put back into the system in a form that other living organisms could use.

The unique marriage of water and land that happens in calm places – estuaries, swamps and tidal mudflats – brought the gift of knowing how to filter water. The ancestors decided to connect a urinary system with genital organs. Hypothalamus, pituitary, and gonads were linked with kidneys. Vertebrates would have a water-filtering system that worked for the assessment and communication of both pleasure and danger. When in danger, these new creatures could generate an acidic inner environment, with corrosive neurochemistry that would freeze their flourishing. Urine would concentrate the ammonia mobilized to neutralize excess acid, and so warn all life around it to press pause. When at ease, these creatures' urine would deliver sources of nitrogen and phosphorous in forms more readily available for assimilation. When in ecstasy, the flow of ejaculate would bring joy to all around.

All the knowledge from plants and insects about how to have a circulatory system was certainly needed. But if these new creatures were going to live long enough to realize the ancestors' dreams, something new had to be added. The major difference between hemolymph (insect blood) and the blood of vertebrates is that vertebrate blood contains red blood cells. The ancestors decided that in these new creatures, the molecular structure of chlorophyll (from plants) could be adapted. Magnesium would be replaced by iron. Both of these metals pulse between quantum states that accept and then unload electron energy. When held in the embrace of nitrogen, in a protective coat of amino acids, both chlorophyll and hemoglobin make tiny beating molecular hearts that power living systems.

Hemoglobin in animal blood and Chlorophyll in plants are amazingly similar in their atomic shape and function. This insight is Diana Beresford-Kroeger's. Drawing by Jcauctkting, Wikipedia, CC.

Even though red-blooded animals are free-living creatures, without roots, iron in their blood means they can always stay oriented. They needed only feel their blood's relationship with earth's magnetic field. Each vertebrate lives inside its own personal, transportable cardioelectromagnetic field, generated by heart muscle pulses, blood circulation, and electrical currents in the heart.

Some bacteria knew how to synthesize magnetite, combining iron and oxygen to make a strong, permanent magnet. Each free-living vertebrate was given this capacity, so they could synthesize magnetite in the hippocampus, the brain area associated with information, learning and memory. Then each being could always stay oriented to the whole biosphere, as it wandered freely. It could choose where to live and how to die, taking stardust to where it was needed, and taking it away from places where it was overwhelming life.

Calcium offered its complex stability. This molecule was already vital to both plants and insects, for structural roles, and for inter-cellular signalling. It could bind with the phosphorus overwhelming ecosystems, and make bone. Vertebrates could concentrate a lot of phosphorus in bones. The transformative magic of phosphorus could stay bioavailable, but be released at a pace that the whole system would have time to integrate.

Throughout its life, each vertebrate would function to break down dead organic matter, so stardust could be made available in forms that other living organisms could take and use. The new system would even allow for the separation of bioavailable nitrogen for short and long-term goals: nitrogen in urine is available quickly, while feces takes more time. Through the first part of their lives, vertebrates would mobilize phosphorus through all their cells and concentrate it in bones. There would be plenty of stardust to mature gametes, and incubate embryos. After reproductive years, there would be time for a gradual releasing of phosphorus, at a pace the environment could gladly welcome. Bones could thin their mineral density from 65 percent to as low as 35 percent, and still support a creature through years of ecstatic aging. If vertebrates lived as well as they would, as long as they could, in place-based communities that honoured their aging and dying, then they wouldn't all die at once. They might even be cherished enough so that each one's ending would warrant tending. Then all the stardust in their dead bodies could be released gradually into the biosphere at a pace that would support more and more life-giving love.

With the pledge of forever by all the fungus and bacteria that could climb aboard to guide each being, and with all learning the ancestors could pack into a DNA suitcase, vertebrates were launched into cycles of living and dying, with the hope that these new creatures could rescue and empower the system.

LISTENING TO DREAMS

We tend to have dreams shaped by capitalism and colonialism. We dream in species-specific language and culture. With awareness of our molecular, metabolic and genetic affinities with every form of life and death, and life-after-death, can our imaginations range more freely? Can we welcome bolder dreams?

Perhaps new ways of being could still be emerging, if we learned to listen to each other, and our dreams. Conspiracies of beings could co-create collective dreams, if we shared our unmet needs and longings in a web of love. Such wild ideas seem impossible – if we only have normal waking consciousness to guide us.

We have learned to attend to only a certain spectrum of energy; our senses "make sense" of the world with selective attention. Hearing, for example, is a capacity to attend and interpret a certain range of energy. The human hearing range is commonly given as 20 to 20,000 Hz, although there is considerable variation between individuals. A gradual loss of sensitivity to higher, faster soundwaves is an ordinary part of aging. Vision is the capacity to discern between different levels of energy, and interpret them as colours of light. The visible spectrum often fades from the view of aging eyes. As we age into less and less engagement with the hypnotic normal, we might find we can better attend to other frequencies and amplitudes of energy that we have hitherto been distracted from noticing. Perhaps we will learn to better attend the inspiring, conspiring stories of our cells, and hear our own and each other's souls. We might better listen to the ancestors' breath, in wind, rocks and trees. With brains less busy interpreting colour, shape and name, we might better understand energy as expression, invitation and relationship.

I imagine we can learn to attune to subtler frequencies of energy, with each others' help. By building capacities for intimacy and true belonging, we may find more space and time to cuddle, stay quiet, and to dream. We can practice making space and time to hear the whispers of cells and souls, inside and around us. We can share psychedelic medicines that help us cultivate expanded awareness and access braver dreams. Dreams conjure new beings and ways of being that guide us home. The interspecies conspiracies called ecosystems are fruitful places to dream in, and co-create our interspecies dreams.

EMBODIED PRACTICE: REACH FOR YOUR DREAMS

Learning to listen to dreams can begin by noticing a sense of protest. Feel how an interaction or observation evokes a sense of repulse, outrage or indignation. Take time to embody your protest. Push away what you don't want. Attend your push, until it finds its outer limit. Keep noticing. Feel your push away turn into a reach for what you long for. It may well be something you have never known. It may be something you don't believe is possible. Perhaps what you want has never been before. At the outer edge of your push, reach for this unknown something. Gather up some threads of it in your fingers, and see if you can pull them closer to you. What is this dream?

EROTIC PRACTICE: CULTIVATE EROTIC DREAMS

Look for common themes, activities or energies that fuel your fantasies. Pay attention to images that evoke a physiological response, despite you. Do you notice any common themes or provocative metaphors emerging? Notice all the people, animals, objects and actions in your fantasy – and consider how all of them may be aspects of you. Are there ways the themes in your erotic dreams have explored you? Are there themes you want to explore more consciously? Can you co-create erotic rituals with intimates, so that dreams and core erotic themes can be honoured, without doing harm?

Tuning in to what real-life desires you can tease out of erotic fantasies is fun. The practice can also help undo any sense we have of compulsively choosing forms of erotic expression that leave us feeling less than whole, or relationship roles we don't want. On the other hand, there is no necessary progression from fantasy to desire. People commonly have erotic dreams that are useful for focusing their minds and generating physiological arousal responses, but they never want to bring their fantasies anywhere near their realities. All these choices are welcome in a world where we consciously cultivate erotic dreams.

DEATH PREPARATION PRACTICE: METAMORPHOSIS

This ritual can be done as a large-scale rite of passage, with the support of guides, medicine and community. It can also be done as an everyday evening orientation to the nighttime world of sleep and dreams.

Create a personal ritual that invites an experience of metamorphosis. Spend some time preparing for the ritual by consciously ending your orientation to acquiring more and more. This reorientation can be both physical and metaphorical. You might stop eating for awhile, stop purchasing and preparing things, and stop orienting to the future. Let yourself feel lost for a little while, as you prepare for the ritual. In your lostness, you might start to notice the emergence of barely-discernable possibilities. Could there be a new version of you, that you don't yet know how to embody? Create a pupa for yourself – perhaps in a hammock in a forest, or wrap yourself up in a blanket in your bed.

Inside your pupal case, let yourself dissolve into a soup of molecules. Imagine all the matter of you has no more shape, longing or purpose. What remains? Are there imaginal cells that offer these molecules a new dream of you?

REFLECTION: WHAT COULD YOU DREAM OF?

What if no dream were too much to hope for? What would you dream?

CHAPTER 11

COMING HOME: CLIMAX ECOSYSTEMS

FINDING MY WAY HOME

There are molecules inside our eyes that are the exact same molecules we began with. From conception, up until a human being is 1-2 years of age, cells in the lens and cornea build transparent, crystalline proteins. These cells are never renewed; the very same molecules stay in them until we die. The crystallins have metabolic and regulatory functions throughout the body. They host the lifelong molecules of our individual souls.

The molecules inside my eyes came together inside a womb that could not welcome me. I was born into a family without competence to care for me, as the oldest of six children in a "nuclear" family. The phrase came into the English language around 1947, two years after the first nuclear bombs were detonated. The metaphor describes our family pretty well, when you add to it the fact that science and society had managed to split the atomic nucleus, creating previously inconceivable violence. Nuclear families were isolated from one another and then, inside each family, everyone was separated by their function. We were lonely and frightened. Sometimes it seemed like all we did was fight. In all the turmoil of our household, we each lived different, terrifying truths. We kept our secrets. We manifested tiny figments and painful fragments of love or freedom. We grasped at scraps of power. My sister and I had a relationship characterized by petty jealousies, deliberate misunderstandings, accidental companionship. Never love. Never intimacy. Nothing to dissolve the space between us. What if we had learned to love each other then? We did not. I did not look for her, look after her. I failed to find what was precious.

Separated by thousands of miles, my sister and I both chose to live as lesbians. We made very different forms of chosen family, with our life partners and our communities. We let our counternormative lives shape our wisdoms and learnings, and the gifts we brought into our work and play. We kept on reaching for each other. Through decades of sharing good-enough love, we found space, time and increasing competence for weaving authentic intimacy. Now I live with deep trust of our foundational love for each other. We help to co-create a loving natal family, as we support our mother on her journey of profound dementia, and live into the challenges and joys of our own aging. We are the lucky ones. We found our way home.

All my life I have been like a salmon, swimming upstream against the current of normative culture, guided by a subtle, insistent knowing that there is a home. Home is a place to rest, a place to play, a place to courageously co-create and defend. Home is a quiet pool within and around me where love is, intimate and true. I know I belong here. I feel a little exhausted and battered by the improbable journey, but I am excited to be with other fish that also feel at home here. We belong to each other, and to this place and practice of counternormative belonging. In this small pond, we can let go of corrosive fear and compulsive helplessness. We can savour our courage, and feel the full aliveness of our differences and their frictions. We can touch each other's bodies and souls, if we want to be touched, building sustained climax states and ecstatic unities.

How does a salmon know there is a home to come home to? How does it recognize home when it arrives? As I reflect on my own experience, I find a sense of homecoming emerges as a felt relationship between my inner imagination and the outer world. I know (or find reassurance) that "It gets better" until my body and being recognize "This is it." When inner imagination and outer world meet and match, I know it in my body. I feel it behind my eyes. I recognize a deep, true welcome home, in the human and nonhuman world around me. It is unmistakable, if I pay attention. And yet, welcome home is not just once and forever. We get messy. We get busy. I change. You change. We fail each other, and disappoint each other. There are continual challenges to belonging, inside and around me.

There is an ongoing experience of home-making, that is a love-making, as I co-create the experience of home. It takes time, and ongoing learning. It takes my courageous willingness to feel my deeply uncomfortable feelings, for all the awful time it takes, until they stretch my compassionate and passionate love to expanded limits. It takes the often invisible, devalued work of emotional labour. It takes commitment to repair, and justice. I am forever learning serenity to accept the things I cannot change and courage to change the things I can. Homemaking also takes a conscious commitment to honouring the limits of learning, the end of making. We need times of sitting down at the table with whatever feast we have managed to conjure in whatever space we have to rest today, to celebrate and savour just this, just now, just us. My experience of homecoming emerges more frequently and intensely as I learn to honour those moments when time runs out on learning. Now or never. This is home! I don't want to miss it.

CLIMAX ECOSYSTEMS

Earth's ecosystems also feel and follow their longings. They attend to arcs of arousal, and manifest extended climax states. They find their way home.

As ecosystems age after catastrophic disturbances, microorganisms, plants, animals, fungi and nonbiotic elements all go through a process of ecological succession, developing over time in place, until they reach a climax state of extended orgasm. For some ecosystems, like fire and flood-dependent landscapes, frequent disturbance is integral to ecosystem development. Other ecosystems, like the wet coastal rainforest where I live, grew old for millennia without catastrophic disturbance before colonization. Coastal conifers live for many centuries. They die and decompose slowly. More than half the total mass of climax ecosystems exists in the form of death: dead trees, crumbling logs, snags and decaying woody material, dead animals. Complex communities of living organisms depend on decomposing material for habitat and sustenance. These forests are a mix of tree ages and species, swamp and rocky outcrop. Innumerable microhabitats support diverse forms of life and death. In the embrace of complex climax ecosystems, many forms of radical uniqueness flourish.

Plants root ecosystems to the earth. Many plants work and play together in the coastal rainforest; the most delicate flowers grow nestled in the roots of the mightiest trees. Other parts of these ecosystems come and go, on different scales and timescales. Amphibians move from pond to forest. Birds fly thousands of miles away, and then return to the exact same grove, the exact same tree, in annual cycles. They are welcomed home with blossoming delight. Young salmon head out to sea as adventurous hunters and gatherers, living in marine ecosystems for years before they bring their harvest home. The stardust they gather through their courageous living into conscious dying gets integrated into all the microorganisms, plants, animals and fungi of their home community. The living and dying of salmon brings ocean's gifts to land-based life through the circulatory system of creeks and rivers, and returns the gifts of land-based life to the sea. There is more home then, for songbirds to come home to, and give the perceptual network of forest ecosystems their long-range aerial view.

Ecosystems around the world emerged as eroded minerals of earth, elements of air, and the excitement of water, together with the molecules of life, made metabolic reactions that broke down some molecules and built up others. Catabolic (breaking down molecules) and anabolic (creating new molecules) reactions would leave lonely particles – charged ions that longed to find new friends. In some of earth's special places, the whole molecular system learned that these lonely ions were a crucial part of the system's magic. By holding lonely, uncompanioned parts as aspects of the whole, with an ethic of "zero waste," these places learned to mature metabolisms with capacity for ongoing evolution and creative partnership. Ecosystem-level metabolism could hold and embody a grounded equanimity,

163

while simultaneously hosting capacity and longing for more. New molecular partnerships could be invited into place-based systems, whose reach for more was not an anxious grab. When charged ions felt wanted inside an ecosystem where they mattered and belonged, the system's reach for more became a resourced and grounded offer or request – capable of attunement: the sub-molecular version of an open hand. Sometimes the open hand of one ecosystem would meet the open hand of another ecosystem. If there were matching longings, these hands could offer and receive caresses, handshakes, or delicious fucks. Soils all around the earth made different forms of life and love this way, separately and together.

Complex climax ecosystems are rooted in soil, where eroded minerals of earth mix with the detritus of the biosphere. When we die, we putrefy. Decomposition disaggregates the stuff of us, and complex molecules called humus form to hold our carbon atoms safe in soil. Humic molecules aren't all the same; there's no universal formula. Simple molecules combine in chains of carbon polymers, making complex macrostructures of different molecular aggregates. A humic molecule is spongy. It can absorb excess nutrients and water, then slowly release them. It can mitigate the impact of toxic elements. Humus occupies a liminal realm between living and nonliving matter. These molecules last for thousands of years in complex ecosystems. But they are also easily lost, when soil is dug up, washed away or broken open. Soil dissolves into acidifying oceans. Carbon flees into the warming atmosphere.

Soils can be lost, and they can also be found. In any complex ecosystem, humic molecules are actively created. Mycorrhizal networks make a sticky substance that sparks coherence of humic compounds. The soil microbial community engages, with up to

10 billion microorganisms and thousands of different species in each gram of soil. Wherever bodies rot, all the different lineages and levels of the biosphere converge and co-create. All that can emerge from death is wanted, cherished, and actively supported in its ongoing becoming.

The Molecular Language of Ecosystems

As the planet got older, ecosystems got more intricate. Their metabolisms generated and integrated the living and dying of individuated beings, and differentiated species. Sometimes one of these beings or species would take more space and time than an ecosystem could willingly allow. There was trauma, violence, and unconscious entitlement. Fear and greed destroyed things. The soil of traumatized ecosystems flew away, and landed in the soil of other ecosystems, and so the soils of earth conspired. Ecosystems around the world realized they needed a communication system that could guide the balance within and between every individuated living thing. They developed molecular messengers, so that each one existing independently could find right relationship between its own needs and longings, and those of the community.[1]

The ecosystems of earth figured out a molecular communication system to guide every being within them, and the relationships between us. Each living and dying body in the biosphere uses this same system. Indolemines, catecholamines,

---

1 Describing the neurochemistry of ecosystems means I am simplifying a complexity that is intricate and intimate. There are hundreds of signaling molecules moving through different domains, phyla, families, genera, and species. Every signaling molecule can have multiple effects, depending on context. By simplifying, and focusing on comprehensible contradictions that particular molecules empower us to embody, I hope to land in some version of emergent truth. This meditation is also included in *Ecstatic Belonging: A Year on the Medicine Path;* it is key to the practices I invite through the free online program at EcstaticBelonging.com.

steroids and peptides are synthesized inside plants, fungi, animals, and some prokaryotic organisms. The humic molecules in soil communicate with each other and the living world through kindred phytohormones. Corresponding neurotransmitters and hormones guide all of our bodies to find serenity, to accept the things we cannot change, and courage to change the things we can.

Ecosystems know that every unique life within them needs to stay grounded in the soil of place, with capacity to be content with no more than what actually exists. It needs to accept constraints on its individual life, and feel respect and self-respect inside those limits. It has to feel empowered to meet its end in a way that honours the ecosystem. It needs ways to feel resourced enough, in living and dying, to keep on offering its stardust back to the whole ecosystem. There are molecules called indolemines that carry this message: auxin, serotonin, melatonin, dimethyltriptamine (DMT).

| DMT | Serotonin | Auxin |

The molecular structure of indolemines.

At the same time, each being also needs to be empowered by something quite opposite to acceptance. Each one needs courage and capacity, so it can live into its longings and bear its agony. Each being needs to be able to assess and endure risk, so it can guard its unique niche in place-based belonging from true dangers. Each one needs daring and desire, to give it strength to rise, and engage in opportunities for both requisite divergence and true partnership. Other molecules called catecholemines – such as dopamine and adrenaline – partner with steroid hormones like cortisol (in animals), brassinosteroids (in plants) and ergosterols (in fungi) to empower courageous and purposeful living.

Adrenaline   **Noradrenaline**   **Dopamine**

The molecular structure of catecholemines.

Ecosystems want and need each one in a community of interbeing to be empowered to accept grief and agony, and still feel longing and joy, so we can each and all stay committed to living and dying in love together. Each one needs to be able to expand into the fierce eudaimonic pleasures of living on purpose, and simultaneously find and feel the contentments of daily care and kindness. Peptide hormones and neuropeptides foster these capacities within individuals, and between all those who touch each other within an ecosystem. In animals, magnocellular oxytocin empowers mad love – risk-taking, passion, impossible somatic openings, like the opening of the cervix before a baby is birthed. It stretches us into the hitherto unthinkable and impossible. Parvocellular oxytocin floods a body with everyday goodwill and welcome, in response to the feeling of belonging, and safe and wanted touch. It lets us savour the sweetness of love, and to act lovingly, with grounded presence. Endorphins manage extremes of agony and ecstasy; they catapult us to a level out beyond ourselves, of transcendent interbeing.

Indolemines and peptides guide us to accept, connect, open and transcend. They resource us to feel belonging fully, and expand into the unthinkable shapes that belonging requires of us. Without these molecules, we might live in a state of emergency, feeling like our personal needs required fulfillment, and self-sacrifice was impossible.

Catecholamines and steroids resource us for courageous engagement with the world. We can cultivate a purpose-driven life, and face the consequent dangers. Without these molecules, we might evacuate our dreams prematurely, or despair of ever even having dreams.

Ecosystems developed this neuroendocrine system that we share with all life, and the life-after-death of humic compounds. Thanks to the signalling molecules within and between us, each being, and the whole conspiracy of beings inside each ecosystem, can better feel and follow our longings for more and better pleasure. We can simultaneously or sequentially follow our contradictory longings, for serenity and peace. Our longings – and the contradictions between them – are trustworthy, when we are anchored in a place and a process that regularly and wonderfully feels like home. Home is the body of each one of us, feeling our resilience and integrity, held in the ephemeral web of belonging that is true intimacy. We can grow into our individuation at the resilient edge of the web's resistance, as we weave evermore belonging for our longings, at the pace of trust.

If catecholamines and steroids get out of balance with indolemines and peptides, we might need the help of culture, community and molecular guides. I certainly need ongoing guidance from molecular medicines, sacred ceremony, and everyday resourcing, to keep on co-creating home. How can I hold the truth of my belonging together with the enormity of my longing? Somatic practices and psychedelic medicines resource us to work consciously and creatively with the neuroendocrine system of ecosystems.

Neuroendocrine System of Ecosystems

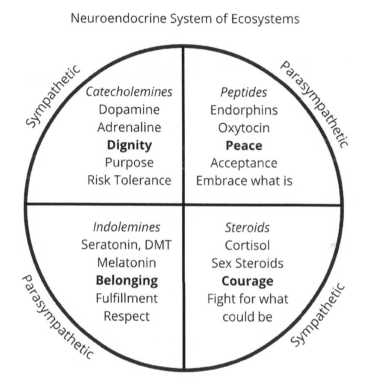

COMING HOME

We feel the force of opposite longings, inside the limits of our bodies, and the limits of ecosystem constraints. We go to the limit, building more and more energy. We want satisfaction, and we want more, and we feel the irreconcilability of our longings stretch us. Then suddenly, energy peaks. We exceed our wildest dreams, and contradictions cascade into new unities. In the bliss of the afterglow, particles and energies flow into new patterns, as we savour.

Orgasm is a complex phenomenon involving mind, body, spirit and emotions. Energy expands, peaks, and is released, accompanied by a sense of pleasure and peace. Experiences of orgasm guide us to right relationship. We can trust the journey of arousal within and between us when we notice how it peaks and ends. The friction between sympathetic and parasympathetic branches of our autonomic nervous system, between ecstasy and equilibrium, engorge and excite us. We build towards climax. Molecular messengers surge and swirl within and between us. They guide us to the place where we know our deep, embodied Yes! As we feel and find the Yes!, and give it our full attention and devoted cultivation, we can make our climaxes more intricate, intimate and transcendent. We can more fully notice those moments when the very thing that all the learning and the longing guided us to arrives. This is it. It is here. It is now. It is within and between us. We are home. Yes! We don't want to miss it.

Dignity, courage, peace and belonging are not empty words. These are embodied states that are felt and experienced. Dignity and courage pull us up into our full height. Peace and belonging stretch us wide. We feel the contradictory pulls: between opposite sides of our nervous system, between opposite tendencies in our attachment patterns, between what's right for me and what works for us. We stretch into even more and better. We offer each other trustworthy, gentle, supported traction, and passionate and compassionate love, so we can stretch just a little more.

Without learning, community and culture, we might forgo the stretch. We might truncate our courage to find belonging, or forgo belonging to preserve our dignity. We might make intimacies small enough so we can meet at the lowest common denominator in our attachment patterns. We could be tempted to hide the agonies in our economy. In social and ecological relationships, we might look to find ease or excitement through privileges assumed at others' expense.

With our individual maturing inside community and culture that resource our learning, we can want and welcome feeling opposing forces stretch us. We will know when and how to devote time to frisky friction, and let the tensions build, until the amplified energy fractures every space of ease within and between us. Our dignity can be engorged, and our courage conjured. We can want, allow and encourage bodies, intimacies, and ecosystems to feel conflicting pushes and pulls, until we reach a climax state of maximum differentiation, and follow small and large orgasmic cascades into unity. We can pay attention to the pleasure of each and every climax, letting the ecstasy of it rock and shape us. In the afterglow, we can savour deep peace, and feel true belonging. This is home.

I live my life in a specific place I call home. Every day I get to thrill with the vibration of resident hummingbirds, and grieve the relentless loss and less of migratory birds, woodpeckers and owls. I lean my heart on and feel engorgement with specific trees who are my lovers and friends. I feel the human ancestors of place, as I live the material benefits that colonization confers on people with white privilege, on the unceded territory of Hul'quimi'num and SENCOTEN-speaking peoples. The big trees have roots that dig down to bare rock left by retreating glaciers through soil laced with evidence of a 10,000-year old Indigenous culture. How do I hold the agony of what this ecosystem could be, and let that recognition continue to shape my purpose and my longing? I want to be a courageous advocate for all that is still possible, with my life and death. And I want to hold my courage and lust for more together with a joyful savouring of what is. This is the home I have always longed for, that I have finally found, and helped to shape. These are the intimate relationships of interbeing I have dreamed of. This is the time of life for me to feel the climax of all my living and learning, and savour my orgasmic enough.

I have worked and played with people who struggle with unintentional ejaculation, and those who are pathologized as anorgasmic. There is a single loving remedy: to pay attention. Pay attention to the arc of arousal, so that we learn to honour our desires, and have them shape our purpose. Attention gives desire space to trust itself, and grow, instead of thinking it needs to go away quickly or be prematurely satisfied. Pay attention to how the world meets you in your desire, and wants and welcomes it, so long as you take only what is gladly given. Feel the engagement, and savour the engorgement, as you fuel your lust for more. Become willing to advocate for your specific lust. Learn to give lust voice, and be convincing, and become deeply worthy of your wanting. Pay attention to the limit of arousal that the unique biophysical system of your body – and any body engaged with your body – can tolerate. See if you can relax there, and spend time at the summit. See if there is a stretch into even more. Then feel and follow the climax. Whatever it is, however it happens, there will be a moment when the time for even more and even better ends. No more learning. No more leaning into the lusting. No more time. Whenever it comes, pay attention. Feel the orgasm. Don't miss it. Don't get lost in wishing it was bigger or better, or that you had more skill, more ecstasy or more time. Take the slide down with delight, and savour whatever bliss you've managed to conjure. Come home, then take time to *be* home. After awhile, explore another arc of arousal, if there is time. Devote temple time to pleasure, where there can be many kinds of orgasm, or none, rather than just engaging until everyone has a conventional orgasm.

The molecules inside my eyes are rearranging, clumping, and starting to cloud a small area of the lenses. These are cataracts, and over time, they may grow larger and make it increasingly harder to see out. This is one of many ways my body is guiding me to feel an approaching end. It is offering me a summit to consciously savour. There is a definite time container on my life, with edges palpable. There is a biophysical frailty I am living into, that forces me to pay attention. My body is guiding me: be home. Bring all your learning to a knowing that time is running out on you. This is it. Now is the time. Say grace. Then don't forget to eat the feast. Celebrate. Savour.

It strikes me that by pushing away the experience of aging and conscious dying, and trying to create a culture that could transcend it, we have finally manifested a biosphere-wide frailty and imminent end. We could try to fix all the ways we are doing it wrong with superficial problem-solving, just like when people numb awareness in order to prevent unwanted ejaculation, or push through vulvodynia to arrive at an approximation of ordinary penetrative sex. We could do that, or we could pay attention. We could listen to our bodies and relationships, and find our way to whatever experiences of sex and orgasm we actually want, and grow capable of wanting, as we learn to listen. We could let each experience of homecoming resource another long-tail of arousal, if there is time.

If there is time, we could grow our desires into more competencies, for generating cultural and economic systems of life-giving, death-accepting love. But when time does run out on us, whether individually or globally, we don't want to miss it. Let's fully feel the climax, as time ends. Let's land completely in the here and now, and enjoy the homecoming, as long as our expanded attention can make it last. The ecstasy of enough and the longing for more both can shape us. If we hold on to each other, in the afterglow, we might just get fused into complex, hitherto impossible new elements.

EMBODIED PRACTICE: MOVING THROUGH THE QUADRANTS

Consider the four quadrants of Dignity, Courage, Belonging and Peace as specific embodied experiences you share with biotic and nonbiotic forms around you. Can you notice ways that a bird, a tree, a wind, a body of water and your own body embody the energies of each of these quadrants? Can you remember a time when you embodied a particular quadrant fully, perhaps at the expense of other quadrants? Or perhaps other quadrants were simultaneously amplified? Make an expression in movement exploring feelings and memories specific to each quadrant. Contemplate how embodying each of these different energies, and the contradictions between them, can guide you in a decision you want to make today.

EROTIC PRACTICE: SELF-PLEASURE

Consider erotic aspects of Dignity, Courage, Belonging and Peace. Devote 30 minutes to a solo exploration of arousal. Integrate a climax. (Your climax can be any form "peak" experience, including but not limited to genital orgasm.) End with five minutes of savouring. Are there times during an arc of arousal where you expand into dignity, or call upon courage? Are there times when you feel deep peace, or transpersonal belonging? Try taking your erotic practice outside, and see if anything changes.

Do the same exercise together with another or others who are also engaged in self-pleasure. Notice whether you relate to your arc of arousal differently, with others present. Do the quadrants of dignity, courage, peace and belonging have different meanings? Are different feeling-states accessible, in the interactive field?

EROTIC PRACTICE: INTERACTIVE TOUCH

Try integrating awareness of dignity, courage, peace and belonging into erotic playtime involving interactive touch.

To amplify dignity and courage:

Amplify catecholemines with purpose and excitement. Set intention together for an erotic playtime where you try something new and a little bit frightening, for a purpose. For example, you might try dressing up, ordering new toys, touching each other in different ways, role-playing, or having sex outdoors, for the purpose of enriching a loving relationship, or inviting more adventurous aliveness. Feel afraid, and take a deep breath. Remember your purpose, and feel fear transform into courageous action. Enjoy the thrill, or giggle at your fail and flail. Savour and rest. Try again.

To amplify peace and belonging:

Amplify peptides with an experience of extraordinary touch that stretches your capacities. Surrender into an experience of requested touch for a given time period (I suggest 30 minutes to an hour). Be sure to have a safe word or stop signal, so you can feel into a joyful stretch without going over the edge, and getting overstretched. You could choose a session of bold sensation that generates endorphins, or a session of soft, slow touch that floods the body with oxytocin. Conclude your session with aftercare that amplifies indolemines, focusing on belonging, respect, and satisfaction.

DEATH PREPARATION PRACTICE:
WRITE TWO OBITUARIES

What if you died today? Take time to write your own obituary. As you consider what to include, remember where in your life you have felt at home, and where you have been able to offer others the experience of home.

Imagine that you have another 10 years to live. What version of yourself, what place, and what friendships do you want to come home to, before you die? Write a new obituary for a future version of you.

Consider sharing this experience with friends you know and trust. Get feedback from each other on what should be included in your obituaries.

REFLECTION QUESTIONS: BODY AS ECOSYSTEM

Consider your body as an ecosystem within ecosystems. What signalling molecules are you receiving, from processes and relationships that bring food and water inside you? Follow your shit into the soil, and your urine into the sea. What signalling molecules are you sending downstream? Tune into your microbiome, holding awareness of the 100 trillion beings that share your body. What signalling molecules are you sharing with the many beings that are co-creating life with you? Consider the human intimacies and communities you are engaged with. How can you cultivate a neuroendocrine environment that feels like home, and welcomes others home?

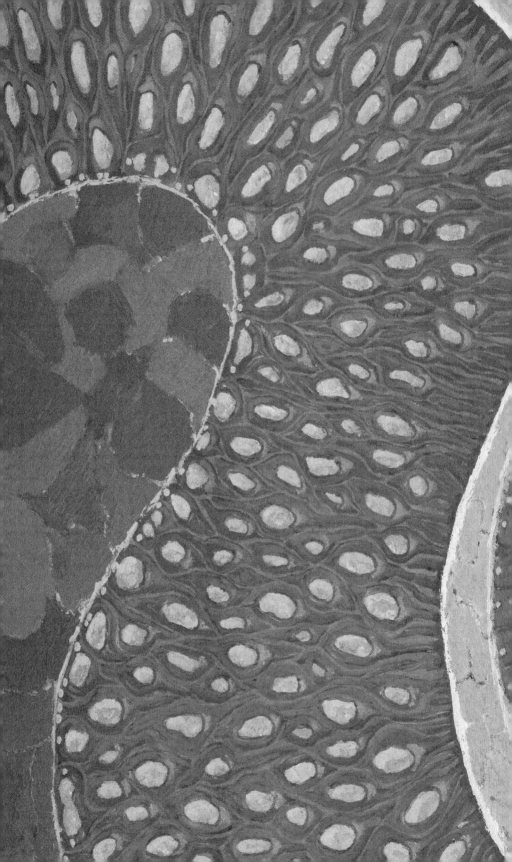

CHAPTER 12

AWARENESS: MATTERING AND NOT MATTERING

Not Mattering

Research reveals how trauma and neglect mute our biorhythms. We experience chronic, low-intensity arousal, with lower peaks and shallower valleys in our levels of stress hormones. The contrast between resting and active heartbeat rhythm is reduced. Excited and relaxed breathing become less distinguishable. Minds cycle in the brain's default mode network, muttering about whatever we are managing.

Muted biorhythms predict danger, and keep us prepared for it. They wisely help us survive another day, so we can find our way home. But chronic muting of our biorhythms has a toxic effect that manifests in reduced lifespan and lower quality of life. Our agonies feel a bit more manageable, but we access less ecstasy. There is never time to fully trust and rest. We don't experience profound peace. We aren't biophysically capable of great courage, and unreserved connection. Our minds are less creative.

Now that I am home, at last, there is no more need to stay muted. I can attend to the joys, and I do. I feel a whole lot of ecstasy. Then, ouch. There is a loss, a helplessness, a rejection, and I land in a whole lot of agony. I am building courage and capacity to really feel it, before I move to fix or escape it, and make it end.

Agony is there for me to feel when I don't matter. I want to be cherished as the one that I precisely am – just me and no other. I am so lucky that, even as I grow old, I am blessed with a whole lot of mattering. But oftentimes now, I just don't matter – even to precious souls who I love passionately and compassionately, even in courageous communities I've helped to co-create. There is no real rejection. I have no adrenaline of outrage to manage sadness with. There is just the agony of feeling a bubble closing, without me in it. People have other priorities. Their world goes on without me. I am excluded, not because I am a target of anyone's negative judgments, but just because I am forgotten, unchosen, unattended and unmissed. As if there was one less fish in the sea. Not mattering.

I've learned to be pretty good at finding ways to matter to both myself and others simultaneously. I've also lived a long lifetime of not mattering, even in relationships and communities where I really wanted to matter. I've already had lots of chances to feel how water closes in around the space where I once was, and I'm not missed. I haven't learned yet to feel patience and passion with it. I've only wanted to resist it. I've used the pain of not-mattering to propel me to find new ways to feel I mattered. Now, as I grow old, I need something different. Surely an important part of aging and dying is finding more and more peace and pleasure in not-mattering, before we end. If I'm only intent on mattering, I'll miss half the truth of getting old. What does matter have to teach me, about mattering and not mattering?

THE COLOUR PURPLE

The colour purple is the threshold-crossing colour on the visible spectrum – it is energy that slows down just enough to get noticed. In doing so, it becomes deeply vulnerable. For awhile, in certain human cultures, purple mattered.

Purple was once so rare it was considered royal and holy. In Tyre, on the shores of the Mediterranean Sea and on the Atlantic Coast of England, there are mounds of mollusk shells, broken in the exact spot necessary to extract a gland containing purple dye.

When all the mollusks with purple in them were dead, purple got even more rare and precious. The people of Europe went off in ships, in search of purple. When they landed on the shores of what's now called Central America, they came upon peoples and cultures that made purple matter in a much more sustainable and joyful way. These people had patience and skill enough to stroke their mollusks, and pleasure them into an orgasmic release of purple. They shared their knowledge, and their carefully tended mollusk beds, with the colonizing cultures. The colonizers didn't get it. They were people in a hurry. They demanded more and more purple. In Costa Rica there was a fierce indigenous rebellion on behalf of mollusks.

The colonizers won control over the mollusk beds, and destroyed many mollusks. But purple escaped. It hid out in cabbages, poppies and ripe plums. It appeared in skies, before great storms, and in engorged organs inside human skins. It kept itself rare and precious, hoping humans would finally get it, and learn to slow down, pay attention, and coax pleasure.

One day, purple got tired of waiting for people to slow down. It decided to speed up. In 1856, it manifested as "mauvine" – a chemically-produced substance that could be used to dye textiles. Purple was patented, and the patent-holder opened a dyeworks for mass-producing mauvine. For a couple of years, between 1859 and 1861, purple was fashionable. Purple hats and dresses were ubiquitous. Finally, with the ordinariness of it, purple stopped mattering. No more fashion, no more wars, no more enslavement and destruction on behalf of purple.

Not mattering to anyone anymore, purple was free. Since nobody cared, it didn't need to stay hidden. On the other hand, it could stay hidden if it felt like it, since nobody missed it. Purple ran around being flagrantly itself, without much impact. It went on teasing and half-hiding too, in transitional moments and intimate spaces. Now it was only folks who stayed curious about the colour purple – even though it didn't matter – who ever learned anything about its power. These curious humans found something quite astonishing. If they were willing to spend time with purple, magic happened. There was an ecstatic threshold-crossing moment, where energy hovered in the transition between visible and invisible, and then landed in the eyes of an observer, and found itself a home. Light became delight.

LAYERS OF AWARENESS

The neurons in a human retina respond to just a tiny part of the electromagnetic spectrum. They respond in two different ways. One type of neuron, called a rod, responds to light, shape and movement. It is highly sensitive, initiating a cascade of molecular consequences from a single photon. Another type of neuron, called a cone, needs more energy to get aroused. Cones respond to colour, and get absorbed in detail. Awareness gets two different information streams about the same phenomenon, with a tiny time lag between them. From our skin, too, there are different neuronal pathways. We get information about being touched from axonal nerves that reach the brain quickly, and from C-fibers that carry the message much more slowly. The same touch is experienced in two different ways, with a time gap between them. There is a sacred pause, and time to consider - what else? What more do I notice? There are also times and places when we don't get that other layer of information. Cones don't see in the dark; only rods are active in nighttime vision. Parts of our body don't have the slower C-Fiber innervation: lips, genitals, palms of hands, soles of feet; we can notice the difference between these parts, and the rest of our skin. By noticing the kinds of awarenesses that are and aren't available to different parts of us, on different timescales, awareness has a way and a reason to get more complicated.

There are many layers of awareness inside us. Each layer operates somewhat independently, at a different speed. Beyond the timescale of vision, and sensation, there is awareness unfolding at the pace of neuronal growth. Is this environment and experience an enriched one, in which the dendrites of neurons grow and reach for connection? Is it an impoverished one, where there is neuronal atrophy? There is awareness unfolding at the level of brain structure. Is this yet more fear, guiding a gradual expansion of the size of the amygdale and a shrinking of the hippocampus? There is awareness unfolding at the level of the neurochemical environment. Is there reason to mute the aliveness and shorten the lifespan of this organism by generating a baseline neurochemistry of toxic stress? Is there sufficient belonging, longing and excitement here, to flood a brain with magnocellular oxytocin, and open a short learning window where everything is malleable? There is awareness unfolding at the level of lifespan, where different learning windows open and close, and can only be opened again with big floods of magnocellular oxytocin produced by high-intensity somatic openings, or chemical allies like MDMA and psilocybin. There is awareness unfolding at the level of salience and relevance, leading to neurogenesis, and long-term memory.

There is awareness unfolding at the metabolic level, as our cells choose how to create energy. There is awareness unfolding at the DNA level, where epigenetic methylation marks impact DNA expression. There is the immune system's ongoing molecular discernments between self and not-self. There is awareness in all the stardust within us, and the subatomic forces they generate between them, that keeps us coherent, and at the same time, keeps us from collapsing into a single particle of matter, and the whole of humanity into a sugar-cube sized bit of matter. All the molecules that make us have distinctive shapes and awarenesses that engender the ongoing dialogue of molecular interactions between them. All this goes on inside our skins. Outside us there are more and more layers and timescales: our intimate environment, the cultural environment, the biosphere, the solar system, the universe…. Each one of us is continually synthesizing a singular awareness from many layers of awareness, inside and outside us. These layers simultaneously unfold awareness of us, deciding how we matter, and when we don't matter anymore.

In all complex systems, different layers unfold on different timescales, as Stewart Brand writing on pace layering guides us to notice. Each layer is functionally different and somewhat independent of the others. It operates with different information sources, at different frequencies and amplitudes, with different influences. Each layer directly influences and responds to the layers closest to it, and to a less immediate and noticeable extent, to the layers farthest from it. Expanding awareness across all the layers, and noticing contradictions between them, while respecting each layer for its particular magic, is what creates capacity for system-level learning and resilience. Complex systems can go on becoming.

New, fast, loud layers grab our attention. Fashion makes a whole lot of noise. Most times, it is forgettable. But if fast, new and loud is held together with slow, old and soft, in differentiated layers, sounds can weave together into a song. Slow, old layers provide foundation. Slow has lots of space in it, but it is not ignorable. Quiet, continuous layers command awareness, over time. Sometimes, fast and fashion make propositions with lasting value. Occasionally, new can punctuate old with radical change.

What is immediate and new grabs our attention. There is an ever-shifting, fast-moving layer of noise. It manifests a whole lot of matter – purple hats, factories, piled up mollusk shells. What is most slow and ancient is not matter. There is the point of zero size and infinite density at the centre of the universe. It is the singularity at the centre of each one of us, where all time ends.

Waves of electromagnetic energy from the universe's beginning are just now arriving, from the oldest, most distant parts of the universe. They vibrate all the particles of us, at a particular frequency. As we each embody the centre of the universe, we have this potency available to our awareness. If we get distracted by all the faster, louder layers in which we matter and don't matter, we could miss out on feeling and forging our entanglement with all of space and time.

WILD MIND

We have brains exquisitely able to respond with critical awareness, to fail and to learn. We learn to speak by babbling, until we learn that only certain sounds have impact. We learn to move by flailing, and then noticing that some movements give us traction and let us crawl. We fail, and thereby learn the rules of belonging in whatever social systems we are navigating. We go through the agonizing, energy-consuming process of learning how to matter. Then we try to keep on mattering. We practice mattering, and we solidify into being what we practice. There is neuronal pruning of unused and disconnected neurons. There is neuronal strengthening of well-used neurons and neuronal pathways. Mattering starts to be habitual – requiring less energy than not-mattering. Our brains settle down into sub-critical rhythms, where failure isn't always so imminent. There is more certainty. New possibilities aren't always urgent and ever-emergent. Awareness devolves into habitual grooves and conditioned tendencies. The brain's default mode network of self-talk, with its focus on rules and roles, dominates our waking awareness. If we struggle with addiction or depression, there is even more inhibition and rigidity. We settle into the sub-critical patterns of mattering, in systems of belonging where we find a fit. But we live in a critical world.

All too soon, we get old, and mattering gets critical again. We make mistakes. We fail, we flail, we babble. We no longer know how to belong. What if, instead of getting triggered into trying harder to matter, we just hang out awhile, getting curious about not-mattering? When we don't matter, awareness can live with much more freedom. With help from advocates of wild wisdom, (for me, these include somatic sex educators, and competent, careful guides of psychedelic medicine journeys) we can rewild awareness. We can encourage our minds to spend time hanging out in the zone of maximum uncertainty. We can make mistakes, try something astonishing, act with courageous purpose, or settle into non-normative routines. We can learn to keep on belonging to each other, and the process.

What we might call "captive mind" – or the brain's default mode network, caught in its ever-anxious rumination about how we matter – is subcritical. What we might call "wild mind" hovers in criticality – where awareness oscillates as far as possible from either rigidity or randomness. At one end of the oscillation, there is increasing excitation. Going any further in that direction would mean there'd be no patterns to discern. No purpose could emerge. There is only random chaos. In the other direction there is increasing inhibition, and habit, until there is no more desire, and nothing ever changes. In the wild awareness of deep uncertainty, as far as possible from both rigidity and randomness, there is so much to explore. Navigating uncertainty is what brains are made for. In the intricate complexity of the neuronal forest, there is multi-dimensional space. Awareness can attend to all the different sounds and rhythms.

Wild mind emerges in wild time, not in the linear narrative that gets generated by how we matter inside the specific social systems we inherit. If our relational world is safe enough to support it, and we can stop mattering for awhile, we can cultivate wild mind. Aging into the increasing truth of not mattering offers space and time to rewild awareness, so our doing and being can emerge from wild mind.

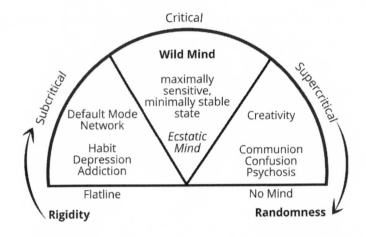

Wild Mind hovers in the critical transition zone between order and disorder. This is where power-law scaling phenomena appear. Drawing made with reference to Carhart-Harris et. al.

BEING AND DOING

In an adult cerebral cortex there are 86 billion neurons, each with thousands of synaptic connections to other neurons. There are as many synapses as there are stars in a universe of galaxies. Neurons generate rhythmic patterns of electrical waves. There is oscillation, at the level of single neurons, local groups of neurons, and different brain regions. If numerous neurons oscillate together, they can give rise to oscillations in a bigger field, connecting local neural circuits to large-scale brain networks.

Neurons have only one kind of electrical synapse. A spike's strength never varies, only its frequency. In the early years of human life, 90% of our neurons get sacrificed, as the brain attends to neuronal fires, and manages their impacts. Neurons join and co-create insulated pathways, to support the flow of all the energy required by doing. Doing gets easier and easier, taking less and less energy. In the brain of an adult, managing habitual doing takes very little energy. New challenges, relationships, tasks, and new lands create new fires. Ever-unfolding emergencies require ever-new mobilizations of the neural network for fire containment.

What happens if, instead of mobilizing all that energy for fire containment, we make just some of it available for the complex, subtle layers of awareness that unfold when a brain is simply being, with nothing particular to do? In the realm of being, neurons have many more choices, connections, and complex ways of communicating with one another than the all or nothing intensity of either On or Off. In the realm of just being, a whole lot of brave, exciting space can open up between On and Off. Where neurons have just one electrical synapse, they have thousands of chemical synapses. There can be a little excitement, or a lot. Uncertainty can grow into curiosity. Curiosity is not commitment. A neuron can change its mind. Diverse connections and disconnections can unfold in time, at different rhythms, for different reasons.

Even if we haven't made cultures and communities with time and space for attending to the subtler layer of being, aging lands each of us in it. Sensory input from eyes and ears diminishes, as vision and hearing impairments offer age-related changes. Stiff hands, painful hips – age-related losses of all kinds reduce our capacity for doing. With age-related "white matter disease," neurons that have been devoted to containing the fires of our doing decide to retire, and so simple, habitual doing takes more and more energy. Increasing dependencies at various levels make novelty less accessible and less desirable. We are stuck with each other. We have to stay home. And so we can – we can choose to – take a break from a lifetime of doing. We can – we must – attend to being.

Taking away the external stimuli of doing from the unimaginably dense and complex network of neurons that exists inside our skulls, we reduce 90% of a brain's normal functions. At first, neurons in areas that are accustomed to managing the fires get noisy. If they are held through their panic, if they can agree to give this other layer of awareness just a little time, something new emerges. The whole neuronal network notices that by taking away the ever-urgent need to attend to fires, we free up enormous amounts of space and energy for neuronal play. The complex ecosystem of the brain has time to unfold all kinds of magic. Waves of profound peace, waves of excited ecstasy, completely new ideas, and newfound choices can emerge, when people spend time in safe-enough, brave-enough settings, just being.

Nothing is Forever: Awareness After Death

The living brain floats in a sea of cerebral-spinal fluid, so gravity barely has an influence, and electromagnetic forces can dominate. Each neuron, and the unimaginable vastness they comprise as a collectivity, trembles in a minimally stable, maximally sensitive state, holding a slightly negative charge. Tiny, local perturbations can propagate through the system at all length scales, leading to fluctuations with lifetimes over all timescales, with a lack of characteristic length or characteristic time leading to maximum diversity. This physical system is exquisitely designed to exhibit self-organized criticality. Brainwave patterns have "pink noise" rhythms, where a long tail of low intensity oscillations gets punctuated by extremely large, infrequent climaxes.

Alpha brainwaves are an exception. Instead of the far-from-equilibrium oscillations of the brain's other rhythms, alpha waves march to their own drum. They are harmonic oscillations, meaning the oscillations that arise when a system is just a little perturbed from equilibrium. Variety clusters in the vicinity of the average. Alpha brainwaves emerge when nothing, in particular, demands our attention, and nothing really matters. For equanimity, all energy has to be equivalent. No more delight, or despair. No more longing, agony and ecstasy. Equanimity is death.

Both the amplitude and frequency of Alpha rhythms decrease - on different timelines - as we age and end. Equanimity doesn't get easier. It is less and less accessible, as neurons grow old together, and are better known to one another, and become more rare and precious. Alpha waves' accessibility, power and frequency can be increased by choiceful equanimity practices like meditation or mindful masturbation; they decrease rapidly with dementia.

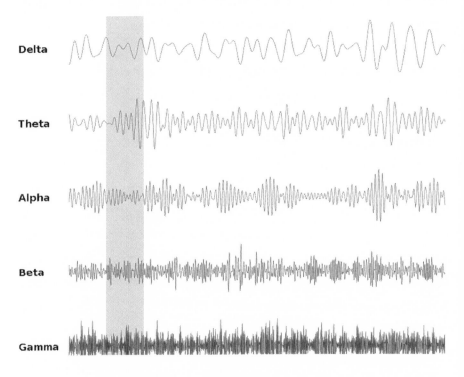

Brainwaves. Ten seconds of simulated EEG data in the five differently named frequency bands of neural oscillations, or brainwaves. Laurens R. Krol, Wikimedia, CC.

When we die, we flatline. The electrical activity of our brain stops being measurable on an EEG, and we are legally dead. I have a story about what happens to awareness after death – resourced by my understanding of brain function and reports of people's near-death experiences. I imagine that when awareness is no longer distracted by all the electrical commotion, it is freed to attend to subtler chemical processes that unfold in the hours or days it takes for an embodied brain to come to an end. If blood no longer brings oxygen, awareness may be anxious at first, and then become more purposeful, as lower oxygen levels spike the production of dopamine. Awareness will likely get more active, perhaps euphoric, as glucose withdrawal amplifies intracellular signalling. Molecules synthesized in dying tissues produce a molecular flood of DMT, even more awareness-altering than the flood of magnocellular oxytocin that initiates our birth. Vivid imagery, and a sense of entering an entirely other world are both likely. As cerebrospinal fluid stops flowing, the molecular residue of chemical processes will settle in the inner aquifer. Pineal and pituitary glands will slowly wilt on their stalks, responding at last to gravity, surrounded by rich molecular soil. Neurons will slowly depolarize, losing their negative charge. Energy depolarization in one neuron will oscillate through the whole system, at first with pink rhythms of self-organized criticality, and then with gradually altered rhythms. Our brain's awareness will approach, and finally settle, in equilibrium. It will know at last that nothing really matters.

Nothing really, really matters, to the universe. Nothing is the web of dark matter that holds it all together. Without dark matter, galaxies would fly apart, or they would never form. Dark matter doesn't absorb, reflect or emit electromagnetic radiation, and so it can't be observed and measured. Yet even with so much uncertainty, scientists say it must exist, or we would not. If nothing didn't manifest with such great density and immensity, energy would have no way to slow down, and no space and time in which to learn how to matter. Pink noise patterns would have no space and time to emerge and intertwine. If there is a cry for attachment from the last neuron in a dying brain, nothing is everywhere, ready to answer. Nothing is forever.

EARTHSONG

We can support each other in letting go of traumatic acculturation and eschewing dissociation, so our biorhythms can come off mute. Growing awareness of sustained and sustaining rhythms in which our lives and deaths are intertwined, we can start to hum along with earthsong.

Earthsong is pink noise: the common rhythm that is ever-unfolding, at different timescales in integrated systems, as a long tail of low intensity oscillations gets punctuated by large, infrequent climaxes. Each octave interval (halving or doubling in frequency) comes to carry the same quantity of energy, over time. Earthquake frequency has the same pink patterns as brainwaves, plankton swarm behavior, and population dynamics in predator-prey systems. Solar flares and orgasms have the same pink rhythms. In every complex, climax ecosystem, pink noise patterns emerge in the distribution of species and in relationships between individuals, species, and the system as a whole. In every organism that can live into a full lifetime, high intensity transformations of birth, early life initiations and critical periods, the long-tail distribution of maturity and aging, and the calamity of death all unfold according to a pattern that aligns us with ecosystem dynamics and the pulse of stars. Every comforting human voice, rainstorm, and every form of music shares pink noise rhythms.

Pink noise patterns only emerge when there are observers with patience and persistence. If we stay aware of subtleties, and avoid dissociation in times of high intensity, we are listening. Great variety would just seem random – if we didn't slow down, remember, and give things time. With patient curiosity, it turns out that great variety is what makes things pink. Rewilding awareness, and coming off mute, we ally our own biorhythms with all these nested rhythms.

As we choose joy, practice peace, cultivate ecstasy, and help each other hold the agony, we sing earthsong. We weave ourselves into the web of life and death, and we are woven.

EMBODIED PRACTICE: BEGIN TIME WITH EVERY BREATH

Wait awhile in the experience of not breathing. Wait until you feel your longing. Let yourself know and grow your desire to go on becoming. Let your longing become more and more intense, and dense, and singular to you. There is only one you. Longing, longing, longing....

Feel the incoming inhalation expand you, as you experience your twinship with the Big Bang that began the Universe and Time. Feel your chest and pelvis expand, and your spine lengthen. Breathe down through your legs and feet, and into your arms and hands. Notice the stardust of you brightening and twinkling, as it experiences the delight of deep receiving.

Let the Universe begin, over and over, with every breath.

Partner Practice

Do the breath practice with a friend, breathing each other's breath. Feel the one you are, and simultaneously explore the us that only you can be, together.

Community Practice

Do this breath in nature, with human and nonhuman community. Let the collective outbreath become a hum, and then a song. Use a call and response rhythm, or create a round, so you can actively breathe each other's breath.

EROTIC PRACTICE: PINK NOISE PATTERNS

See how it feels to cultivate the erotic by taking your erotic energy off mute, and exploring a pattern of long-tail, low arousal energy with infrequent, high-intensity orgasms.

Throughout the day, let a trigger (like going to the bathroom, or reaching for a snack) remind you to tend your erotic aliveness. Breathe deeply into your pelvic floor. Use your hands and/or your imagination to invite arousal. Take a few seconds or a few minutes welcoming arousal, but stopping short of orgasm. Notice whether you can enjoy arousal without needing to either repress or express it.

If you do this several times a day, every day, you may begin to notice erotic energy informing your everyday lifeworld, in joyful and surprising ways. See if living with a long tail of low arousal impacts the intensity of your orgasms, when you do choose to enjoy a climax.

DEATH PREPARATION PRACTICE: LIFE, BREATH, DEATH

In a safe-enough environment, cultivate equanimity brainwaves. Spend some time meditating on a mountaintop, floating in a bathtub, or finding another way to support yourself in a practice of just being. Clear your mind and focus on your breath. Occasionally, stop breathing, noticing any emergent awareness.

REFLECTION QUESTIONS:
FOR INDIVIDUALS, INTIMACIES AND COMMUNITIES

Mattering and Not Mattering

List ways that you matter and don't matter. Notice where not mattering destabilizes energy, or frees energy, within or around you.

Complicating Awareness

Can you find ways to deepen awareness of old, slow energies and new, fast energies, while filtering awareness of mid-range norms? Walking in the forest, can you stop to notice a tiny, delicate flower, and then again to notice the long-range mountaintop view? In lovemaking, can you spend more time in the long tail of low, slow arousal, and also reach for experiences of intense ecstasy? In social and economic life, is there awareness of deep, slow processes that cohere and decohere relationships as well as awareness of current crises?

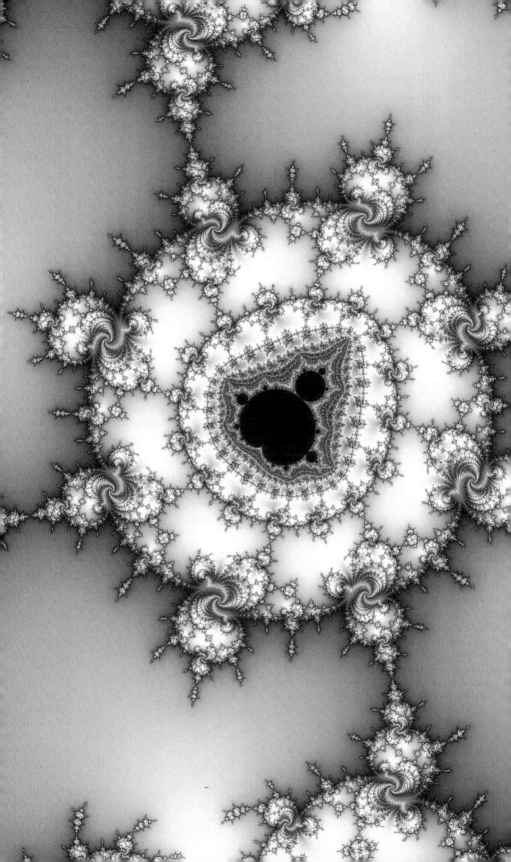

CHAPTER 13

MATH OF THE
IMMORTAL SOUL

SOUL-TENDING

I have been lucky enough, and patient and curious enough, to find companions who coax and care for my shy soul. In the delight and despite of enduring intimacies, my soul knows what it is to feel cherished. I have experienced soul-deep ecstasies, and true communions. My soul has found its voice, and been heard. My soul has also found its challenges. There are too many times, even at my age, when it gets locked in mortal combat. Resentments, obsessions, distractions, traumas and heartbreaking conflicts have almost extinguished my soul, and they go on threatening to steal my soul. Some days, soul just knows it has gotten way too old for this. It is too battle-scarred and weary to carry on.

But as long as I go on choosing not to end it, there is space and time to feel the harmonies and dissonances, simultaneous and sequential. Soul is discerning. It can hear its music. It can notice when the music ends. This pointless, weightless, ever-uncertain part of me recognizes resonances, as they emerge from harmonies. It can learn to sing better, and listen more carefully. It can practice – though never be perfect – finding rhythms it can dance to, as terms of engagement change in committed relationships. My decades in recovery rooms, my erotic friendships, my work as a sacred intimate, the magic of queerness, and my journeys with psychedelic medicines have all been resonant music for my soul. I've learned to dance, and notice when I stumble and fall. I've been able to feel my soul become both purposeful and playful. And even with all the uncertainty and complexity that emerges whenever I look into a soul, there is one thing I know for sure: some part of my soul's purpose, and its playfulness, is touching other souls, and letting them touch mine. Ay, there's the rub!

There is the rub, the frisky friction, the interplay of ecstasy and equilibrium, the dream and the nightmare, now and forever, because then it's not just the music of my soul that matters. It's feeling and finding how to weave my resonant music with your music, at your soul's timescales, according to your rhythms. Sometimes it really works, and sometimes it really fucking hurts. Sometimes conflict is generative, opening fractal dimensions between either-or options where love and life can go on unfolding. Sometimes we really hit the limit. Worlds diverge. Parallel universes peel apart, so they can get away from each other, and be forever unknown to each other. Sometimes separation means needing more distance. Maybe for now, maybe forever. The ongoing discernment, of what is or is not rectifiable, is what opens up a field of infinite (or no more) space and forever (or no more) time that is the field of the soul. Zero is a magic number, half real and half imaginary. It needs patient, curious souls to tend it.

Without You, I'm Nothing

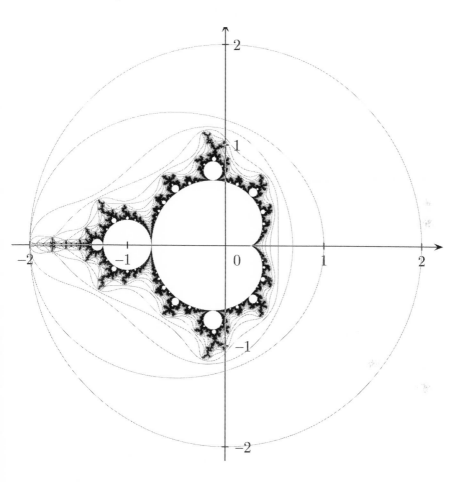

Plot of the Mandelbrot set. Shown are the lines between areas of different iteration counts to exceed the boundary value 2. Axes of the complex plane are drawn from -2 to 2, where the real value rises from left to right, and the imaginary value rises from the bottom to the top. Geek3, Wikimedia, CC.

Before the beginning of time, when all was potential, there was neither something nor nothing. There was just zero – half real, and half imaginary – because without something, how can nothing exist? Without nothing, how can something exist? To exist at all, you have to be something: something real, something discernable. There has to be a point. A point, however small, is not just clouds of uncertainty. It is a vulnerable, measureable something. Wave functions diverge, irreversibly, as points emerge from them.

Points can only emerge when there are observers to make them. Someone has to resist the infinite irregularity of neither-nor with some discernment. One soul has to be willing to hover at zero, imagining less and noticing more. Once there is a point, then there is always someone to miss it, and someone to get it. Someone will argue that something is better than nothing or nothing is better than something. To exist at all, the universe needed a few brave souls, willing to see the point of potentials. There had to be a conspiracy of souls, to coax just four dimensions to unfurl.

It took four – no less, no more – of many possible dimensions, to make a universe where matter could gather in communities of eager observers, keen on their points. If there was only one dimension – breadth – and points diverged, they would go on getting farther and farther away from each other, without hope of reconciliation. Unfolding a second dimension, of height, means there are options for circling round, and second chances. A third dimension, of depth, makes even more pathways for convergence and divergence – points can travel round and round or go straight on through. Then large communities of points can converge, and structure three-dimensional bodies with insides and edges, where gravity bends space and that makes time.

Unfurling dimensionality is risky. Unfurling together with other dimensions makes things even more vulnerable. As breadth, height, depth and time unfurl in enduring relationships with one another, each dimension feels its difference and finds its limits. There are some irrevocable decision-points, where a thing has to be either up or down, in or out, here or there, now or never. Irreconcilable differences mark boundaries of maximum divergence. Fractures open up in inter-dimensional spaces. A profusion of possibilities emerges in degrees of freedom between each dimension and the others. More and more points can go on emerging in inter-dimensional spaces. Souls can go on making points matter, through their learning and loving. There is space where souls can have bodies, and soulful relationships can have time.

As all this something emerges, so does a whole lot of nothing. There are discernable limits, where everything ends. Zero appears again, 13.8 billion years older and wiser, but still half-real and half-imaginary. For zero to exist, it still needs souls that can hover, imagining less and noticing more. To tend and cultivate the zero field, souls need wild imagination and capacity for bold sensation. Souls have to be willing and able to notice and imagine irreconcilable differences between something and nothing. Before time began, the differences between something and nothing were relatively easy – almost-inconsequential aspects of the discontinuous structure of neither-nor. After 13.8 billion years, time and space have grown a whole lot of difference between point and potential. There is so much to lose, and so much to miss.

The Mandelbrot fractal is a representation of what emerges from iterative consideration of interactions around zero, mapped to points of interest in space, given iterations in time. What emerges is an ongoing discernment between what is and is not rectifiable. What is rectifiable circles and cycles. At some irreversible point, there is no point; it goes to zero. What is not rectifiable seeks escape. If it gets strong enough, it exits the zero field, and heads for infinity.

With enough iterations, we can see that zero is an attractive point: near numbers head there. One is a repulsive point: near numbers want to get far, far away. Between zero and one there is room for argument, but zero always wins it. It's all rectifiable; it all comes to nothing in the end. It is just outside of the obvious differences between something and nothing, in the imaginary field of less than zero and more than minus 2, that enormous complexities and uncertainties emerge. There is another fertile space of resistance, between more-than-1 and less-than-2. Iterative considerations of these points yield places where small differences have enormous impact. There are discernable points of no return, between what is and is not rectifiable, that go on ever-unfolding. Some differences cunningly resist extinguishment, and escape into infinity. Differences between all and nothing are ever-emerging, at various timescales. Patterns are always recognizable, yet always a little bit different, in ways that are neverending.

If souls are bold and curious enough, there is immortality in the tending and defending of the zero field. In the repeated imagining and discerning of differences between all and nothing, souls can hitch a ride to infinity. And this is actual infinity – not just really big, like this particular universe. It is actual immortality, not just 'til the end of time. Moreover, this is no meaningless, featureless infinity, just something or nothing, where souls' refined capacities for ongoing discernments are scarcely needed. This is an infinity of evermore beauty and mystery, that the ongoing, nuanced discernments of what is or is not rectifiable are actually manifesting. Patterns of infinite variety go on emerging and diverging, at every size and timescale, by way of immortal souls' making the iterative inquiry, and seeing the points of divergence. Without the ongoing discerning, there would be no infinity unfolding its evermore intricate complexities. The inquiry and its answers manifest an escape hatch from the imminent, vulnerable limits of space and time.

ZERO FIELD OF DIVERGING WORLDS

Schrodinger's cat. Conceptual illustration,
Andrzej Wojcicki, Science Photo Library

Physicists say that all of being is half-real and half-imaginary, at once measurable point and ever-indiscernible uncertainty, both particle and wave. Physical systems don't have definite properties, independent of whether those properties are discerned. Matter exists as moments of certainty we harvest, from a field of possibilities and probabilities. Our very discernments are what make particular points, and worlds that go on, and evolve in time.

In the 1920's a physicist called Schrodinger imagined a thought experiment that anyone who has ever loved a cat finds truly terrible. He imagined putting a cat into a box, with a device that releases poison through radioactive decay. Because radioactive decay happens all at once, and unpredictably, the passage of time brings no certainty. So long as there is no one deciding, divergent worlds are still actual. It's only when the box gets opened that possibilities collapse into certainties. An either-or moment unfolds. The cat is either alive, and leaping from the box to snarl and purr and play again. Or the cat has died, alone and unseen, with all its capacities for love and life cruelly, senselessly ended.

In the 2020's there is a biosphere where the same experiment is being hosted on a massive scale. All life of earth is in a box, with poison being released in such a way that no measure of time is meaningful for predicting an imminent end. Everything is still actual. Every outcome is still imaginable. The cat is both alive and dead, as alternative possibilities evolve simultaneously.

With enough iterative inquiry, we can't help but notice: the irrevocable consequences of cruel experiments and ugly imaginings go on unfolding the particular future they have determined. Whether it's this cat or that, now or soon, the consequences of so much hatred and fear add up. They are not rectifiable. They escape into infinity. We can't help but notice, too, that so much life-giving love, beauty and meaning have made a world of profound consequence. We can take time to feel the irrevocable truth of this, still unfolding, in our bodies, cells, atoms, energy and relationships – in all that is precious.

When souls get the point of all the love and longing, at so many levels around and inside them, truth emerges from clouds of uncertainty. So many shared discernments can't be demeaned or diminished, and made to come to nothing in the end. Love adds up and escapes into infinity.

We can dare, then, to open the box, eager to see the cat, with flashing, angry eyes, and bristling fur. We open the box with hands that know – or can learn – how to care for the cat, and coax the complex vibration of purrs that we can nest our own vibration in. We open the box, because we want to find and relish the so-called poison of the molecules and their radioactive decay. We can enjoy – or at least endure – the decaying old molecules telling their stories, again and again – those same old stories we know so well, and already embody. We open the box, because we understand it's the box itself that makes poison out of such good medicine. And even the box, once it's broken open, and sitting empty, can be a thing we learn how to love.

The zero field, where immortal souls are discerning the difference between what is and is not rectifiable, is where divergent worlds peel apart. Immortal souls need to choose, then, which world they want to go on with. If we go home with the one that brought us to the dance, we choose love.

LIFELINES: NOW AND FOREVER

How long is a life?
It's all relative.
Where are we standing?
How fast are we moving?
How small is the increment of measure?
What parts of life get counted,
in the way we measure time?
Does the now that is me begin at the beginning of time,
when the matter and energy of me emerged?
Or in the death of stars,
when the molecules of me were birthed?
Or in the conspiracy of molecules

that learned to hold and harvest energy,
so they could live in love together as a biosphere?
Or at conception,
when my DNA diverged?
Or at my birth, when the placental web
that empowered my becoming reached its limit?
Maybe I begin right now,
as all the past converges
in a moment
with irrevocable impact on the future.
Maybe I begin at my death,
when the sum of my life
ripples out from all I was,
through space and time.

We can notice that, when it comes to time, you cannot put too fine a point on it. The smallest possible increment of measure that can be imagined into existence is still a point, and points add up into lines, and lines mark limits. If now is a point in time, it is a point of no return. But if there is no point, if now is a measureless nothing, then a fissure fractures the zero field. The fracture makes loopholes, and then there are slits where archers can stand at the ready. Souls can hold time's arrows, poised to tend and defend their communities. If an arrow is shot through the loopholes, time can interact at one point, irreversibly with other points, and simultaneously propagate through space like a wave, bending around corners, being in two places at once.

A point in time, however small, has density. If you add enough points together, you get a timeline, with a beginning and an inevitable end. This is the arrow of time that knows the difference between past and future. The arrow has already been shot; it is going somewhere; it has velocity. You can't go back in time; there is an irreversible direction. The arrow has mass and edges. It is subject to gravity. To understand time as an arrow, we need memory. We need points that add up, so we can feel their shape, and notice their impact. We stand outside time, to see its shape and trajectory, and observe the sequential unfoldings. We hope and remember. An arrow can kill enemies; it can save intimates. It can harm animals; it can feed a village. It can fall flat and miss what it's aimed at. Arrows have integrity and edges; they can be broken.

Inside the arrow of time, there is a porous and discontinuous world, where there are hundreds of thousands of cells, and 100 trillion atoms inside each cell. In the wood the arrow is made of, there are ongoing processes of decay, fungal life, desiccation and erosion happening at slower timescales. At the scale of a millionth millionth of an inch, there is a quantum world of infinite intricacy. Differences between matter and energy barely exist. Limits are ever-uncertain. All points are arguable. A particular, particulate now is ever-arriving, from every possible path. Its impact goes on, into every possible future. Ancient and ever-new exist simultaneously. The zero field between now, never and forever is ever-unfolding. There are many worlds, inside time's arrow.

In the practice of sacred intimacy, we enter and co-create a time-inside-time. I describe it as "temple time," and imagine it was an awareness cultivated by *horae* – priestesses of the hours and sacred whores of the ancient Mediterranean Sea. Temple time opens an otherwise inaccessible spaciousness. The intensity of energy is amplified, as frequency slows down. We can make temple time in devotions to erotic pleasure. I find it in communion with plants, on psychedelic medicine journeys, and through song. We come into an intricate world, where particles that feel like an arrow from the outside are somehow, sometimes also waves. Waves vibrate particles, and there is music.

This is good work and play for the old and grey: to live and love each other in temple time. As we slow down, we can slow time down, and infinitely expand it. We make time inside time, with our choices, attention, and our loving touch, with our intimacies and ecstasies. Forever can go on existing, even while we hold an equally true awareness that the arrow of this time, our time, has an irrevocable trajectory, an origin and an imminent end.

EMBODIED PRACTICE:
THE ZERO FIELD OF BEING AND NON-BEING

Find a body-temperature medium in which to float, in a lake, bath or hot tub, imagining no boundaries. Let your awareness of skin dissolve as you become water, and water becomes you.

EROTIC PRACTICE: BOTH-AND PENETRATIONS

This exercise can be done with any orifice, body part, or toy, alone or with another or others.

Spend time hovering in the zero-field that is the half-real, half-imaginary edge of you. Engage in an erotic experience that helps your body and soul open to experiencing penetrating and being penetrated simultaneously. When you are ready, and wanting, welcome deep receiving into your singular self. Really notice yourself being penetrated. After awhile spent experiencing penetration, see if you can use the sensation to help you grow an imaginary penetrative organ. Imagine your inner world extruding, and yourself penetrating another. After a few minutes spent experiencing penetrative energy in your imagination, go back into the actual experience of deep receiving. Use imagination and sensation to pendulate between penetrating and being penetrated.

DEATH PREPARATION PRACTICE:
CONTEMPLATING THE ZERO FIELD

Watch a video of the Mandelbrot Fractal, and then unfold a contemplation of your own soul's navigation of the zero field.

Consider harm done. We have all had harmful impacts. We have all been harmed. What is true for you? What is and is not rectifiable?

Consider how love won. Contemplate the many times you chose love, offered love, made love and discerned it. What are the consequences of love, that are still unfolding?

If you have another day of life, are there ways you want to reach into the curve of time, to rectify and repair? Are there ways you can better acknowledge what is and is not rectifiable?

See the "Apology Ritual" and other resources in the "Belonging to Repair" chapter of *Ecstatic Belonging: A Year on the Medicine Path.*

REFLECTION QUESTIONS

Discerning Love

Is there a way you can commit more fully to the ongoing practice of discerning love? What are you grateful for? Who do you care about? How can you cultivate more and better love, in all your relations?

Temple Time

Is there a way you can regularly explore the time-inside-time's arrow? Try consciously creating or co-creating a dedicated ritual time to share stories, explore touch, honour ancestors, eat a meal. Notice how differently an hour can pass in the experience of temple time. How can temple time-inside-time resource you, your intimacies and communities?

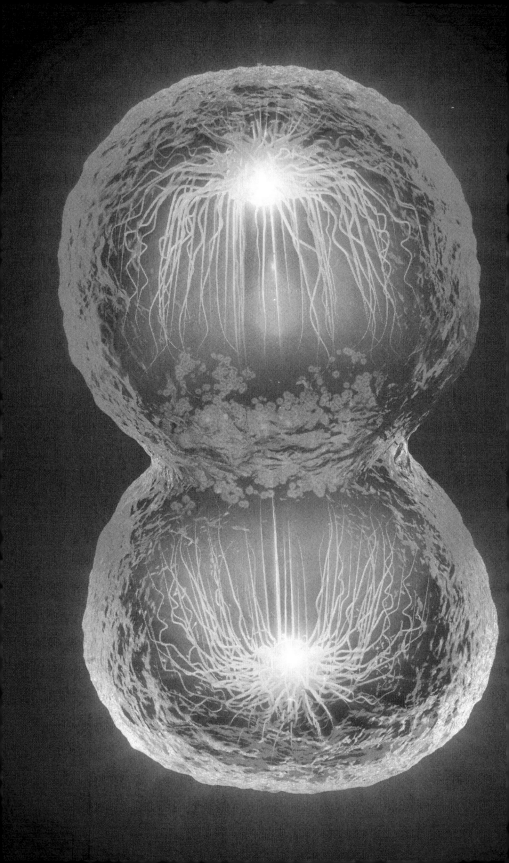

CHAPTER 14

THE HAPPY END

BEING WITH DYING

I realized a few years ago that my time of being in primary partnership with other humans was done. I still have committed, intimate, erotic relationships. Indeed, I can love more fully and freely than I have ever been able to love before, in this time of life when I do not need to manifest shared finances, co-housing, and other everyday lifeworld forms of meaning and mattering. I can just love and be loved, in the ever-changing rhythms we find for weaving an ever-evolving us. Primary partnership, for me, is something different. I've had two such partnerships in the human realm. The first, with a man I partnered with from age 17 to 27, was woven with incompetent true love. We tried to cherish each other's cells and souls, but when our needs diverged, too much bitter conflict emerged. That partnership ended. My second partnership was with the woman I wove life with for 31 years, Mearnie Summers. Through all our many adventures, co-creations, differentiations, radical shifts and impossible-to-metabolize challenges, we became and remain partnered. Our cells and souls got entangled by living and dying together, in some primary, fundamental way, so that one of us cannot be fully described without considering the other.

I don't want another human in that place again. Instead, I try to weave my primary entanglement with Lover Earth, happy to be one among many who hold her as their primary partner too. A few years ago I spent three summer days in ceremony – with the companionship and priestessing of my dear friend Greta Jane – to mark my commitment. I had rings made from the diamonds and gold I had worn to symbolize my human partnerships. I buried one, and I wear the other as a symbol of my vows - to love Earth, in all her infinite intricacy and gender queerness, to have and to hold her, to be fully had and held. I pledged to cherish and be cherished by her, and that I will let our partnership open me and fill me up, and keep on growing into my own best becoming inside her. I promised to make love, and take love, until death unites us even better. I vowed not to be distracted by longings for belonging or dignity that would have me forsake her, and myself, and the glow and pulse of our giving and receiving.

Lover Earth and I live together, and she holds onto me, despite my imperfect learning about how to be a good partner. I try to understand her love languages, and offer words of appreciation, devotions of time and money, and my comforting and exciting touch. I want her to feel truly, deeply, creatively loved.

When I had a human partner, I was her advocate. I am called to advocate now for Lover Earth. I feel her still so alive, passionate, courageous, strong, and infinitely complicated. Anything could happen. And I feel the frailty. She is experiencing the unravelling of the non-equilibrium systems of her uniqueness. There is not a lot of time left. Momentum is gathering for a series of catastrophic failures and a final, critical state change that will be the very end.

I am guided by my decade-long experience of being with Mearnie's dying. At first I resisted. There were multiple crises, surgeries and hospitalizations. Eventually I came to understand her dying as a process I could not reverse. I could comfort, care, grieve and witness. I could partner. And I did that, through many more years of her slow decay, punctuated by numerous crises, almost-endings, and ongoing escalations in our systems of care. We were well-supported in finding daily pleasures, and weaving competent true love, through our last years together. But sometimes I felt stretched way past my limits. I felt her dignity demeaned, as being bedridden, and needing intimate help with every basic body function, would strain and sometimes shatter the underresourced systems of care we were able to mobilize. Some days, there was not enough patience, kindness, money and energy.

When the last few days of Mearnie's dying finally arrived, I had a hard time believing it. We had been through so many crises of almost-dying, so many times before. But a nurse with fierce courage and kindness helped me understand that this would be the end. And so I was able to hold Mearnie, and companion her transition, and be in loving entanglement with her living, all the way through those last days of her dying, and past her end.

I felt resourced. I knew something about how fear and love dance together in our bodies, from my own trauma and healing. My experiences of journeying with sacred plant medicines seemed to guide me, so I could hold being and non-being together, and be a bridge. I had help enough, so I could notice when I was losing presence, get support to have a break, and return refreshed.

Helping Mearnie be with her fear was a big part of it. She was afraid of failing me. She expressed fear that she would no longer be able to look after me. I held her in her shock, lonely grief and then relief, in learning I was okay with her dying. She came then to a different fear. She struggled for words to share it, and finally found breath enough to say her name: "Mearnie Irene Summers." The words were just right to describe the witness we were in, of letting go of this unique being who had never been before, and who would never be again. We were at the end of a time that began with the very first cell of her, and added up, moment by moment, year by year, to now. Her beloved body was coming to an end. We held that fear together, for hours. Mearnie wanted to be conscious and stay with the process, as long as she could have her eyes locked to my eyes and be loved. I sang to her. There was medicine enough, so pain and fear didn't get too noisy. I kept on holding her, as her body went on failing. She experimented with not breathing. We hovered in the maybe and maybe not. Then there was one last exhale, and a final decision. No more Mearnie Irene Summers. No more embodied weave of us. I held her, as her body cooled, and the molecules settled and shifted.

There were hours, after her death, I wanted to be with her body. There were months after her death, I wanted to be alone. I needed time and space enough to be in curiosity and uncertainty, grief and relief, numbness and brand newness. For something new emerged in Mearnie's death that had not been before. We forged a new kind of quantum entanglement, through the process of being with dying in love together. When I had time enough with the brand-newness, I could weave it into my ongoing becoming.

Now I am partnering Lover Earth, in this time of her dying, while I feel into my own aging and imminent end. I want the brand new entanglement that can only be born through conscious dying in love together to exist, in whatever comes after. I want to be part of a competent system of care that helps some of us do this.

THE END OF TIME, THE LIMIT OF LEARNING

Climate chaos, the rise of fascism, global capitalism and a global pandemic… it seems that we live at the end of time. The 4 billion years of learning that made the biosphere is at the edge of ending its perfectly imperfect unfolding of life-giving love.

Time is an artifact of being, in the way we know it, through learning systems that age and inevitably end. Learning is a non-equilibrium system. It begins and matures, through tests, traumas and trials. At the organism level, ecosystem level, and biosphere level, there are patient and ruthless teachers, guiding us towards the unquestioned goal of learning: how to have more time. We learn to find the longest-possible place and pace of dynamic stability. Learning creates more time for the pleasures and challenges of living into our uniqueness, and the uniqueness of the systems of life-giving love we partake of, delight in, and defend. Uniqueness belongs to time; it is terminal.

Timelessness is a property of nonbeing. A brain intent on being cannot learn it. But in temple time, in conscious dying, we can start to feel and find it. The gates of grief, terror and awe are there to guide us. Ecstasy opens the door to it. After Eros, past the realm of meaning, in the disaggregation of our terminal uniqueness, we can feel its spaciousness. With purpose fulfilled as best we can with what we know, time ends. We enter and become nonbeing. There are no more irreversible processes with

219

time direction. We are Chaos, emptiness and nothingness; we come into a place before and after our becoming.

Timelessness is where unpredictable change might or might not occur. Patterns of great beauty and complexity emerge unpredictably from Chaos, and then, there is Eros; there is something to love and lose. In the longing for more time, time begins. Love is the reason for learning, and learning can only happen if and when it matters. If there is only rigid stability, there is nothing to learn. If there is only random chaos, learning doesn't matter. But when patterns emerge, and are discerned, then there is need and reason for learning, so as to hold the beauty with enduring love, and gain more time. Each time that time begins, it creates a linear time that will age and end, and then open again into timelessness – but it will be timelessness made more intricate and enormous by its intercourse with time. Chaos will not be only formlessness and emptiness; it will host new elements.

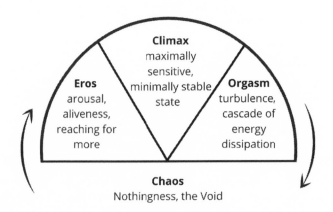

LIFE AFTER DEATH

There were many big bangs before the one that began the universe. Maybe a 100 trillion times, through timeless time, big bangs produced matter and antimatter in equal amounts. They cancelled each other out, leaving behind pure energy. Time stopped before it began. Matter's longing to matter had to mature some courage and self-respect, before singularity could emerge as an organizing force.

The subatomic particles of us all have ancestors that longed to matter, but they had no time and space in which to mature a capacity to matter. They met their end in an orgasmic encounter with antimatter in timeless time. The ancestor particles that learned how to matter were those who loved their longing enough to endure their agony. They contained their longing inside shapes with edges, so their desires could reach out from their centres, feeling for a fit. Then particles could attract partnerships with other particles, that had matching longings and competencies. And so hadrons, atoms and stars could be born, and matter could exist in enduring relationship with antimatter.

The particular stardust of earth's matter matured even more capacity for life after certain death. It survived the spectacular explosion of a giant star that could have ended it. The end of our ancestor star could have disaggregated all its matter into pure energy. That sometimes happens, in the death of stars. But inside our ancestor star, there was matter that reached out to other matter to create relationships that could survive the end. Together, this matter gathered up the energy of the dying star into itself, and forged complex, hitherto impossible elements: carbon, nitrogen, oxygen.

Out in space, in the vicinity of the exploded star, these complex elements held on to their self-awareness. They kept on moving fast enough to resist collision and derision in relationships that were wrong for them, until they found each other, and joined with other elements with matching capacities and longings. Then they could aggregate into the dream of a planet, without annihilating each other. Together, they made a shape with edges. They gained velocity and gravity enough to find a home inside a solar system. As a beloved planet inside a stable solar system, the elements of earth grew old in love together.

There is memory of all that has ever happened to earth, in its atoms, aggregates and elements. The original stardust let itself be changed. Complex new elements were forged, as earth felt caresses on its crust, and had its hot, wet longing shared and deeply penetrated. Sedimentary rock was formed from small particles of rock or stone, compacted by pressure, while other rocks were weathered and worn. Living organisms contributed shells and bones. Earth made its partnerships of enduring, exciting love. It was sometimes stripped of them. Since the Cambrian explosion of multicellular life some 550 million years ago, five mass extinctions have stripped earth of vast systems of life-giving love. A sixth and largest-ever extinction event is now ongoing. Animals, plants, fungi, ecosystems, social systems, nervous systems and weather systems all are experiencing relentless daily violences, catastrophic losses and agonizing ends. My soilless human ancestors are discernably responsible.

In the presence of so much death, I find it comforting to reflect on how even atoms die. We all have innumerable, mortal radionuclides inside us. And with each death of every atom, 5000 times a minute, new energy is born. In the multiverse generated by quantum effects, hidden worlds diverge. These ever-diverging parallel worlds are similar, but not the same. Maybe in some of these hidden worlds, there is a kinder kind of capitalism. There might be a slower, gentler climate catastrophe unfolding, that some forms of life could go on evolving in. There might be one last chance to change things. These worlds are similar, but not the same.

But what if, every little once in awhile, there is a conspiracy of atoms, reaching beyond their personal ends to connect with the field of atoms dying around them? What if they let their own individual ending synchronize and resonate with others' endings? Could waves of energy emitted from multiple deaths empower otherwise-impossible changes? Could conscious dying be generative of something otherwise unknowable? Could it initiate an antiparallel world, where love wins?

PREPARING TO DIE

Civil rights activist John Lewis described how anti-racist activists in the 1960's would prepare to embody the principles of non-violence, in marches, demonstrations and a way of life that exposed them to constant, mortal danger. How did these activists become biophysically brave and resourced enough resist their own cowardice, in the face of monstrous, deadly violence? How did they metabolize the corrosive effects of constant threats, from thugs and authorities, and mobilize courage enough to show up for even more dangerous engagements? How did they look into the eyes of hate, and feel the crunch of the bludgeons that could end them, and still embody nonviolent, life-giving love? They learned how to do it. They prepared to die, while embodying what they cared about. Death preparation takes training, study and practice. They studied the principles of nonviolence, and they practiced what facing death would feel like, in safe-enough, brave-enough ways, in loving community. They trained with theatre in which white people faced contempt and violence, and learned to toughen up the neuroendocrine fragility their white privilege had engendered. They built their biophysical capacities for dying with integrity, through courageous, imperfect practice. They sang together, and the music and thrilling words that resonated through all the singers singing wove connection and commitment. Their bodies had space, time, training and resource, so they could learn courage. There was vibrational support, so souls could grow in the experience of resonance. In their messy and imperfect learning, these activists lived the dream of beloved community.

The Happy End

If you are still with me after all these words, you know I love a good story. And every good story deserves a happy end. Here's the happy end I can imagine.

There are few old trees left to guide us. But there are more and more old humans. The global human population is aging exponentially. As we prepare to die, grounded on the common ground of earth, we can't help but notice the different trajectories of love-guided time and fear-guided time, as these two different timelines simultaneously unfold the fate of the biosphere. What if, in our own ecstatic aging and conscious dying, we choose love? What if we live the dream of beloved community, in our imperfect trying?

On the line of linear time, basic laws of physics are applicable. You can't make or destroy energy. The total energy of an isolated system remains constant; it is conserved through time. Energy doesn't die or get born; it can only be transformed, from one form into another. But as Schrodinger himself reminds us, statistical laws of physics are just probabilities in a field of infinite variety. That means there are moments, places and processes where these laws are completely contradicted. The particles and energies of us have already broken all the rules. They know how to do this. They have already manifested the impossible, in the birth of the universe. Life is impossible. Cellular replication is impossible. Meiosis is even more impossible. Major evolutionary transitions can't happen, but they do.

Watching a cell do the impossible, with cell replication, there is a process that unfolds in time. The molecules feel and find synchronization and vibrational resonance. The helical structures of chromosomes – that loosely unfold in the other phases of the cell cycle – compact into tight coils, and line up in perfect rows, like synchronized swimmers with in line with other chromosomes. When at last the synchrony and amplified vibration reach a just-right resonance, the molecular machinery pulls out the stops, and a cell undergoes an ecstatic threshold-crossing surrender. It dies into the two different things it is becoming.

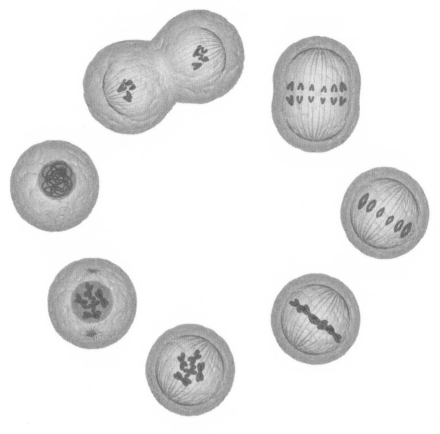

Cell mitosis, Canva

Synchronization is an emergent property that occurs in a broad range of systems, on multiple scales. Even inert objects like pendulum clocks evolve sympathetic synchronizations with one another, mobilizing quantum-level oscillations through a common ground to support synchronized movement. By moving together, they generate and integrate an otherwise inaccessible energy. Humans unconsciously synchronize footsteps, heart rates, respiratory rhythms, and hormonal cycles. We feel and follow each other's pulse. We match deep, pelvic breath. With time, trust, and common ground, we align. Synchronization emerges in abrupt transitions of autonomous oscillators. Full synchronization emerges from very little synchronization via a non-linear system, as additive feedback loops generate sudden, transformative change.

Resonance is another energy-generating system. We can hear, feel and find a quality of sound vibration that emerges, when we embody the contradiction between resilience and integrity. Resonance is deeper and different from harmony, and yet it requires harmony to unfold. A resonant frequency excites a system to vibrate with more energy than when that same force is applied in disharmonious environments, or with other, non-resonant frequencies. Small periodic forces that are near enough to the resonant frequency of a system to not overwhelm it have the ability to produce large oscillations in the system. Interactions between resonant frequencies allow for the generation and storage of vibrational energy.

Just as it takes time and learning to coax a violin string to resonate, or one voice, or a choir, each resonant system needs time and space to learn just how. All learning begins with babbling. There is chaotic motion, then self-organizing systems emerge, and there is reason and capacity for discernment. When I was a teacher, I would listen for resonant voices – a quality of prosody that emerges as students begin to trust themselves in a network of trustworthy relationships. Now I am old, I can focus on attending this thing I call resonance in all my intimacies. I have an undeserved grace and space in my life, so that I don't need relationships to manifest more social belonging. I can just try to feel and find how I can nestle into the resonant vibration of a beloved. There are messy mistakes and imperfect learnings. But if we keep on feeling our way, listening deeply, and following our longings, there can be more and more attunement. There can be threshold-crossing moments that open into extended periods of enjoying just-right resonance with another, where we explore and cultivate whatever Eros is unique to the weave of us. My resonance with another can bridge life and death. It is amplified by wanted touch. It can be non-local.

In each atom, in every cell of life, in every individual life, in each ecosystem, social system and solar system, there is a longing for resonant relationships. If we let our longing exist, and give it our attention, it will guide us home. Curiously holding and unfolding capacities for resonance that are embedded in our atoms, cells and souls, we can keep on learning. We can reach for the capacities that 13.8 billion years of learning have already matured, in all the quanta of us: submolecular particles and energies; atoms; molecules; cells; soils; souls. We can find resonance with the dying biosphere.

OUT BEYOND IDEAS

Out beyond ideas, there is a field we walk alone. One or nothing? Before and between each choice for breath, where we say Yes to the one we are, there is Maybe. Is there reason to expand into one, from nothing? Is there longing? Is there resource? With each breath we say Yes! to the one we are. Each death is a choice for No.

We live in a social context where breath is policed and privileged by relentless systemic inequities and monstrous incidental violences. Can we open space enough inside and around us, to explore the Maybe field within us? When we hang out in the field between Yes and No, energy vibrates. There are tremulous, low amplitude waves of uncertainty, close to the No. There are large-amplitude waves of excitement, close to the Yes. There is amplified vibration, as difference emerges, between the non-equilibrium system of one, and the equilibrium-driven system that is the sum of everything (which, without one, is nothing).

Between two different ones, even more Maybe emerges. Each one can better feel its own charge, shape, gravity, velocity, frequency and amplitude, in relation to another. There is an ongoing discernment of whether we do or do not fit. If we get courageous enough to be curious, and not quite decide yet, we can play in the inquiry, and give it spacious time. We can see if there is rhythm. Is your pulse happening at a pace that I can dance to? We can explore whether there is pitch. Can I simultaneously listen to the one of me, and notice you? Does my sound and your sound feel clear and stable enough, in relationship with each other, so as to be distinguishable from noise? If there is agreement on pitch and rhythm, we can explore making music. We can notice the peaceful consequence of consonance, and we can rest there. We can notice the friction of dissonance – how it disturbs and ignites us. We can learn how dissonance that is too much too fast will disastrously end us. But if there is too little dissonance, too long, we fade into silence. When there is interplay between consonance and dissonance, we can amplify aliveness. We can learn to comfort and delight.

Consonant frequencies, stacked vertically, open space for resonance. There is sympathetic vibration. The experience of resonance between us opens more resonant space within us, and we can bring that back into the weave of us. Dissonant frequencies, contextualized in a vertical harmonic pattern, make chords that want to move forward, climax and cascade into satisfaction, and ease. Climax, given attention, can be sustained – but not forever. Savouring satisfactions makes for conscious, transformative ends, with seeds of brand-new beginnings in them.

Resonant relationships are generative. They open new dimensions of me and you. They let us settle into the singularity I am and you are, and co-create the just-this-one of us, that we can only be together. Singularity, anchored in a resilient web of authentic belonging, gets deepened in its dignity. Belonging, manifested through intricate intimacies between singularities, gets evermore power and truth. In our cells, souls and relationships, we live into the process through which the universe goes on emerging, and the biosphere goes on becoming.

When we feel synchrony and resonance, two is more than one plus one. We exit linear time, where addition is simple. We bid goodbye to the heteronormative world of either-or. The weave of us is more than the sum of us. Energy unique to us is generated, within relationship, because of relationship, just as happens at every level of existence. Like hadrons, atoms, molecules, cells, ecosystems, and the solar system, we conspire. The flow of energy within and between us generates a field of magnetic force around us, to attract and repel energy. Reaching out from the truth of enhanced stability and empowerment, we can feel and find our way to other resonant intimacies, and communal ecstasies. In the weave of an ever-evolving us, we generate power.

Resonant relationships can grow resonant systems that engender vibrations of a specific frequency. Resonant systems act as filters, picking out specific frequencies from a cacophony of complex vibrations containing many frequencies. A resonant system knows and grows itself in the experiment of feeling frequencies that are too much and not enough vibration to be resonant. By holding the process of ongoing discernment inside it, the system creates an oscillation that amplifies its energy.

With resonance, we contradict the laws of physics. We open spacious time, within just-this-one moment that will never be again. There is time inside time then, for a sacred pause, wherein the field of Maybe can emerge at another level.

In the sacred pause, we have time to wonder: Will there be more time for the biosphere of life-giving love to go on becoming? Or is this time's end? We can feel the tremulous waves of almost-nothing, close to "Time's run out on us." We can feel the large-amplitude waves of excitement, close to "Yes, together we can." There is amplified vibration, as the difference between Yes and No emerges with our noticing. We can feel the friction of contradiction between the non-equilibrium system of life-giving love, and the equilibrium-driven system that is the end of everything.

Dare we follow a longing
for even more love, and even more time?
Dare we feel how that same longing
organizes the atoms, cells, souls and soils of us?
Have we capacity to hold the terror and the grief?
Have we courage?
Have we companionship?
In the weave of us, each death can say Yes!
to what we dare to dream of.
We can commit our ends
to beginning the brand new things
that are otherwise impossible.

The biosphere has witnessed many mass extinctions. We are made of learning and loving that has survived them. We already know how to cultivate the biophysical courage we need, to live and die with purpose, inside the extinction event that is currently unfolding. Like the stardust we are made of, the soil we stand on, and our cells, we can orient to ecstasy and savour equilibrium. We can live our lives and die our deaths in commitment to enduring love. With resonance and synchrony, we can generate energy, and use it to transform the predictable into the otherwise impossible. Like the molecules we are made of, and the biosphere we embody, we can contradict the laws of physics, and co-create a happy end.

EMBODIED PRACTICE: SACRED PAUSE

Learning to take a sacred pause, and amplify the energy of Maybe, are ideas I draw from Betty Martin's Wheel of Consent. This suggestion for embodied practice comes from her work.

With a friend, create a three-minute game structure to explore asking for wanted touch. Take turns asking each other, "How would you like to be touched?"

Receive the question and take a breath. Don't answer right away. Take a sacred pause, and hover in the Maybe. Notice all the history, expectations and inhibitions that could keep you from knowing what you want, and asking for what you want. Consider all the rejections, capitulations and appeasements fear seems to require of you. Notice how your habits shape you. Notice your concern that anything you request might be judged to be too much, or too little. Then notice your longing. How do you long to be touched, in this moment, by this person? Courageously request a touch you long for.

As the person asked to offer touch, don't leap into doing what has been requested, or saying No right away. Take a sacred pause, and ask yourself, "Is this a gift I can give with full heart?" Hover in the Maybe. Notice all the ways you habitually say either Yes or No. Notice how you have had to please and appease others, and fight their incursions.

If you cannot give the requested touch with full heart, say No. Notice how hard it is to say No, but refrain from apologizing. As the person requesting touch, notice how hard it is to hear No. Then thank the person for their courage. Say, "Thank you for taking care of yourself."

When you find an authentic request that can be met with an authentic Yes, receive wanted touch that is offered with a full heart, for three minutes. Then reflect on the experience.

Taking time in the Maybe can help us find a Yes or No that is more authentic, and less reactive or habitual. We become more true to ourselves, with time in the sacred pause.

How could you bring this embodied experience of hovering in the Maybe into a death preparation practice? Are there ways you see the whole world hovering between love and death, exploring the Maybe?

EROTIC PRACTICE: SACRED PAUSE

Do the Sacred Pause exercise naked, integrating possibilities for whole body touch. If you enjoy the inquiry for three minutes, expand it to ten minutes for each person. Try a 30-minute game.

EROTIC PRACTICE: SACRED PAUSE BEFORE ORGASM

To build biophysical capacity for manifesting courageous new worlds, we can spend time at the cusp of orgasm. After building arousal to the edge of climax, stay awhile. This practice is also called edging. Explore how you can do this best – each person is different. We might find a sacred pause by shifting the fantasy a little. We might change a pattern of sexual stimulation, slightly, just before we orgasm, or make subtle shifts in breathing patterns or muscle tension. Feel yourself fall back into lower states of arousal, then reach for more, finding the edge again (and sometimes again and again). Time spent hanging out in the sacred pause can sometimes yield very intense, extended orgasms. Sometimes arousal fades, or orgasm becomes inaccessible.

DEATH PREPARATION PRACTICE: REHEARSE THE END OF THE WORLD

Co-create a ritual rehearsing the end of the world.

Who do you want to be with, at the end of the world? Where do you want to be? What do you want to be doing, when the world ends?

REFLECTION QUESTIONS

How are you feeling the relentless daily violence of the mass extinction currently unfolding? (Numbness is a feeling.)

Are there ways that you can resource your nervous system and social system by preparing to die, in the service of what you value?

Considering the fate of the biosphere, what seems impossible, and yet, feels deeply longed for? Have you collapsed your longing prematurely, because it seems impossible to get what you want? Does it help you dream your impossible dreams, when you consider how the universe itself is impossible?

Consider resonance, and feel and find places, people, poetry and practices that feel deeply resonant. Notice how your own vibration is amplified, in connection with resonant frequencies.

LET'S MAKE MAGIC

There is a method to magic.

People focus on what they value; they see what they expect to see. Expectations impact observations. Predictions pull specific outcomes out of a superposition of possible truths. But there's a gap between what's predictable and what's inevitable. It's there that magic can be made.

By eschewing ordinary values,
and working in the gap,
one magician can learn
to pull a rabbit out of a hat.

Many magicians together
can ensure that capitalism and colonialism end.
Love wins.
The biosphere can mend.

I have to believe: we are magic. We are the dreamers, rule-breakers and love-makers who co-create this queer universe. Eschewing ordinary values and any attachment to the predictable, we can work and play together in the gap – so the impossible can suddenly emerge.

Acknowledgements

I go on learning and discerning the path of embodied love within a web of love. I feel woven with the more-than-human world. I am held in a broad cultural web, where two great teachers – who are also friends – especially resonate as I write today. Daniel Elliott is a Stz'uminus Elder, art-maker, author and healer. Kai Cheng Thom is a storyteller, teacher of somatic sex education, and creator of the Loving Justice methodology. They both seem to embody love, in all they do. There are many other culture-makers whose work embodies love, and invites my love to grow. For example, I do not know Karine Bell or Alixa Garcia, but I feel called to share these words with you, because their words sang to me.

My web of love is also deeply intimate. I want to especially acknowledge Doug Wahlsten. This book began in our conversations exploring the science and art of aging. It was patiently tended, for years, in the caring container of our trustworthy love. Liesbeth Van Rompaey was an early reader who offered invaluable guidance. Barry Carl was a muse for this project, and a supportive ally. Sophia Faria served as a creative and caring editor, who convinced me to jettison over half of the manuscript. Other friends – including Wendy, Tom and Marnie Baxter, Claire Rubach, Corinne Diachuk, West, Noah Kloze, Greta Jane, Paula Stromberg, Kristan Huthmacher, Christiane Pelmas, Anne Zeller, Debbie Louise, Dee Larsen, Max Tea, and Tricia Bowler – all walk the path of embodied love in their own beautiful ways. My friendships with these extraordinary humans help me find my way.

Though I have retired from teaching, I continue to explore ideas, find inspiration, and share embodied love with old and new friends in the field of sacred intimacy and somatic sex education.

I am so grateful each and every erotic friend – client, colleague, student, intimate. I have irreplaceable friends I will never meet, yet we touch each other: through our ways of being, and with our words. We meet through the common ground of earth, and through the internet. In quantum-level oscillations, we can feel and find our resonance. I cannot be me without the love we make. What we co-create is true and holy.

Bibliography

1000 Genomes Project Consortium, Auton A, Brooks LD, et al. A global reference for human genetic variation. *Nature*. 2015; 526(7571):68–74. doi:10.1038/nature15393

A new insight into how DNA is held together by hydrophobic effects (Update) [WWW Document], n.d. URL https://phys.org/news/2019-09-dna-held-hydrophobic.html

A New Theory About the Structure of DNA | Cell And Molecular Biology [WWW Document], n.d. . LabRoots. URL https://www.labroots.com/trending/cell-and-molecular-biology/15723/theory-structure-dna

Aid, F., 2019. Plant Lipid Metabolism. Advances in Lipid Metabolism. https://doi.org/10.5772/intechopen.81355

Aken, O.V., Clercq, I.D., Ivanova, A., Law, S.R., Breusegem, F.V., Millar, A.H., Whelan, J., 2016. Mitochondrial and Chloroplast Stress Responses Are Modulated in Distinct Touch and Chemical Inhibition Phases. Plant Physiology 171, 2150–2165. https://doi.org/10.1104/pp.16.00273

Aldaz, S., Escudero, L.M., 2010. Imaginal discs. Current Biology 20, R429–R431. https://doi.org/10.1016/j.cub.2010.03.010

Al-Lamki, R.S., Skepper, J.N., Burton, G.J., 1999. Are human placental bed giant cells merely aggregates of small mononuclear trophoblast cells? An ultrastructural and immunocytochemical study. Hum Reprod 14, 496–504. https://doi.org/10.1093/humrep/14.2.496

Armbruster, W.S., Muchhala, N., 2020. Floral reorientation: the restoration of pollination accuracy after accidents. New Phytologist n/a. https://doi.org/10.1111/nph.16482

August 23, M.S., 2012, n.d. The Cosmic History of Life-Giving Phosphorus [WWW Document]. livescience.com. URL https://www.livescience.com/22641-cosmic-phosphorus-first-life-astrobiology.html

Ball, Philip. The Self-Made Tapestry: Pattern Formation in Nature. Oxford University Press, 1999

Beggs, J.M., Timme, N., 2012. Being Critical of Criticality in the Brain. Front. Physiol. 3. https://doi.org/10.3389/fphys.2012.00163

Burleson KO, Schwartz GE. Cardiac torsion and electromagnetic fields: the cardiac bioinformation hypothesis. Med Hypotheses. 2005;64(6):1109-16. doi: 10.1016/j.mehy.2004.12.023. PMID: 15823696

Beresford-Kroeger, Diana, The Global Forest: Forty Ways Trees Can Save Us, Penguin Books; Reprint edition 2011

Bhat, S.P., 2003. Crystallins, genes and cataract. Prog Drug Res 60, 205–262. https://doi.org/10.1007/978-3-0348-8012-1_7

Bisaz, R., Travaglia, A., Alberini, C.M., 2014. The neurobiological bases of memory formation: from physiological conditions to psychopathology. Psychopathology 47, 347–356. https://doi.org/10.1159/000363702

Blankenship, R.E., 2010. Early Evolution of Photosynthesis. Plant Physiology 154, 434–438. https://doi.org/10.1104/pp.110.161687

Brain Waves - an overview | ScienceDirect Topics [WWW Document], n.d. URL https://www.sciencedirect.com/topics/agricultural-and-biological-sciences/brain-waves

Brand, S., 2018. Pace Layering: How Complex Systems Learn and
   Keep Learning. Journal of Design and Science. https://doi.
   org/10.21428/7f2e5f08

brown, adrienne maree, *Emergent Strategy: Shaping Change, Changing Worlds*,
   AK Press, 2017

Brumos, J., Robles, L.M., Yun, J., Vu, T.C., Jackson, S., Alonso, J.M.,
   Stepanova, A.N., 2018. Local Auxin Biosynthesis Is a Key Regulator
   of Plant Development. Developmental Cell 47, 306-318.e5. https://
   doi.org/10.1016/j.devcel.2018.09.022

Buckberg, G.D., 2002. Basic science review: The helix and the heart. The
   Journal of Thoracic and Cardiovascular Surgery 124, 863–883.
   https://doi.org/10.1067/mtc.2002.122439

Cadwallader, A., Lim, C., Rollins, D., Botrè, F., 2011. The Androgen Receptor
   and Its Use in Biological Assays: Looking Toward Effect-Based
   Testing and Its Applications. Journal of analytical toxicology 35,
   594–607. https://doi.org/10.1093/anatox/35.9.594

Carhart-Harris, R., Leech, R., Hellyer, P., Shanahan, M., Feilding, A.,
   Tagliazucchi, E., Chialvo, D., Nutt, D., 2014. The entropic brain: a
   theory of conscious states informed by neuroimaging research with
   psychedelic drugs. Frontiers in Human Neuroscience 8, 20. https://
   doi.org/10.3389/fnhum.2014.00020

Chialvo, D.R., 2010. Emergent complex neural dynamics. https://doi.
   org/10.1038/nphys1803

Chamovitz, Daniel, *What A Plant Knows: A Field Guide to the Senses*, Scientific
   American / Farrar, Straus and Giroux, 2017

Choi, C.Q., n.d. Strange but True: Earth Is Not Round [WWW Document].
   Scientific American. URL https://www.scientificamerican.com/
   article/earth-is-not-round/

Carroll, Sean, *Something Deeply Hidden: Quantum Worlds and the Emergence of
   Spacetime*, Dutton, 2019

Cytoskeletal Dynamics During Cytokinesis [WWW Document], n.d. URL http://celldynamics.org/celldynamics/research/cytokinesis/index. html

Dansereau, D.A., Lasko, P., 2008. The Development of Germline Stem Cells in Drosophila. Methods Mol Biol 450, 3–26. https://doi. org/10.1007/978-1-60327-214-8_1

Delmont, T.O., Robe, P., Cecillon, S., Clark, I.M., Constancias, F., Simonet, P., Hirsch, P.R., Vogel, T.M., 2011. Accessing the Soil Metagenome for Studies of Microbial Diversity

DiLoreto, R., Murphy, C.T., 2015. The cell biology of aging. Mol Biol Cell 26, 4524–4531. https://doi.org/10.1091/mbc.E14-06-1084

DNA "dances" in first explanation of how genetic material flows through a nucleus [WWW Document], n.d. . ScienceDaily. URL https://www. sciencedaily.com/releases/2018/10/181025113156.htm

Doerner, P., 1998. Root development: Quiescent center not so mute after all. Current Biology 8, R42–R44. https://doi.org/10.1016/S0960-9822(98)70030-2

Donovan MF, Bordoni B. Embryology, Yolk Sac. [Updated 2020 Mar 29]. In: StatPearls [Internet]. Treasure Island (FL): StatPearls Publishing; 2020 Jan-. Available from: https://www.ncbi.nlm.nih.gov/books/ NBK555965/

Eagleman, David, *Livewired: The Inside Story of the Ever-Changing Brain*, Doubleday, 2020

Elert, Glenn, Music and Noise, The Physics Hypertextbook, https://physics. info/music/

Elphick, M.R., Mirabeau, O., Larhammar, D., 2018. Evolution of neuropeptide signalling systems. J Exp Biol 221. https://doi. org/10.1242/jeb.151092

Eme, L., Spang, A., Lombard, J., Stairs, C.W., Ettema, T.J.G., 2017. Archaea and the origin of eukaryotes. Nature Reviews Microbiology 15, 711–723 https://doi.org/10.1038/nrmicro.2017.133

Fabrizio, P., Longo, V.D., 2008. Chronological aging-induced apoptosis in yeast. Biochim Biophys Acta 1783, 1280–1285. https://doi.org/10.1016/j.bbamcr.2008.03.017

Freestone, P., 2013. Communication between Bacteria and Their Hosts. Scientifica (Cairo) 2013. https://doi.org/10.1155/2013/361073

Gibney, E., 2017. Photons pair up like superconducting electrons. Nature News 550, 438. https://doi.org/10.1038/nature.2017.22868

Goodenough, Ursula , *The Sacred Depths of Nature,* Oxford University Press, 1998

Gomez-Lopez, N., StLouis, D., Lehr, M.A., Sanchez-Rodriguez, E.N., Arenas-Hernandez, M., 2014. Immune cells in term and preterm labor. Cellular & Molecular Immunology 11, 571–581. https://doi.org/10.1038/cmi.2014.46

Graham, N.A., Tahmasian, M., Kohli, B., Komisopoulou, E., Zhu, M., Vivanco, I., Teitell, M.A., Wu, H., Ribas, A., Lo, R.S., Mellinghoff, I.K., Mischel, P.S., Graeber, T.G., 2012. Glucose deprivation activates a metabolic and signaling amplification loop leading to cell death. Mol Syst Biol 8, 589. https://doi.org/10.1038/msb.2012.20

Grillo, Marco, Jordi Casanova, Michalis Avero, A Deep Breath for Endocrine Organ Evolution, Current Biology https://doi.org/10.1016/j.cub.2013.11.033

Hamilton, T.L., 2019. The trouble with oxygen: The ecophysiology of extant phototrophs and implications for the evolution of oxygenic photosynthesis. Free Radical Biology and Medicine, Early Life on Earth and Oxidative Stress 140, 233–249. https://doi.org/10.1016/j.freeradbiomed.2019.05.003

Hawking, Stephen, *A Brief History of Time: From the Big Bang to Black Holes*, Bantam-Dell, 1988

Heidstra, R., Sabatini, S., 2014. Plant and animal stem cells: similar yet different. Nature Reviews Molecular Cell Biology 15, 301–312. https://doi.org/10.1038/nrm3790

Höhn, A., Weber, D., Jung, T., Ott, C., Hugo, M., Kochlik, B., Kehm, R., König, J., Grune, T., Castro, J.P., 2017. Happily (n)ever after: Aging in the context of oxidative stress, proteostasis loss and cellular senescence. Redox Biology 11, 482–501. https://doi.org/10.1016/j.redox.2016.12.001

Humphreys, Claire P., Peter J. Franks, Mark Rees, Martin I. Bidartondo, Jonathan R. Leake & David J. Beerling, Mutualistic mycorrhiza-like symbiosis in the most ancient group of land plants, Nature Communications volume 1, Article number: 103 (2010)

Hood, S., Amir, S., n.d. The aging clock: circadian rhythms and later life. J Clin Invest 127, 437–446. https://doi.org/10.1172/JCI90328

Hordijk, W., 2013. Autocatalytic Sets: From the Origin of Life to the Economy. BioScience 63, 877–881. https://doi.org/10.1525/bio.2013.63.11.6

How Do Single-Celled Organisms Have Sex? - The Atlantic [WWW Document], n.d. URL https://www.theatlantic.com/science/archive/2020/11/how-do-single-celled-organisms-have-sex/617072/

Hoyle, G.L., Steadman, K.J., Good, R.B., McIntosh, E.J., Galea, L.M.E., Nicotra, A.B., 2015. Seed germination strategies: an evolutionary trajectory independent of vegetative functional traits. Front. Plant Sci. 6. https://doi.org/10.3389/fpls.2015.00731

Ingram, G.C., 2020. Family plot: the impact of the endosperm and other extra-embryonic seed tissues on angiosperm zygotic embryogenesis. F1000Res 9. https://doi.org/10.12688/f1000research.21527.1

Iriti, M., 2013. Plant Neurobiology, a Fascinating Perspective in the Field of Research on Plant Secondary Metabolites. Int J Mol Sci 14, 10819–10821. https://doi.org/10.3390/ijms140610819

Johnson, Ayana Elizabeth. "What If We Get This Right?" On Being with Krista Tippett, https://onbeing.org/programs/ayana-elizabeth-johnson-what-if-we-get-this-right/

Kenneth Jones and Tema Okun, "White Supremacy Culture," from *Dismantling Racism: A Workbook for Social Change Groups*, https://www.thc.texas.gov/public/upload/preserve/museums/files/White_Supremacy_Culture.pdf

Kaartemo, V., Akaka, M., Vargo, S., 2017. A Service-Ecosystem Perspective on Value Creation: Implications for International Business, in: Value Creation in International Business: Volume 2: An SME Perspective. pp. 131–149. https://doi.org/10.1007/978-3-319-39369-8_6

Khamsi, R., 2005. Carbon dating works for cells. Nature news050711-12. https://doi.org/10.1038/news050711-12

Kimmerer, Robin Wall, Braiding Sweetgrass: Indigenous Wisdom, Scientific Knowledge and the Teachings of Plants. Milkweed, 2013

Konkel Lindsey, n.d. The Brain before Birth: Using fMRI to Explore the Secrets of Fetal Neurodevelopment. Environmental Health Perspectives 126, 112001. https://doi.org/10.1289/EHP2268

Kropotov, Juri D. Age dynamics of alpha rhythms Data from Human Brain Indices (HBI) database, Functional Neuromarkers for Psychiatry, 2016

Kutscher, L.M., Shaham, S., 2017. Non-apoptotic cell death in animal development. Cell Death & Differentiation 24, 1326–1336. https://doi.org/10.1038/cdd.2017.20

Lasocki, S., Gaillard, T., & Rineau, E. (2014). Iron is essential for living!. Critical care (London, England), 18(6), 678. https://doi.org/10.1186/s13054-014-0678-7

Lancaster, M.A., Knoblich, J.A., 2014. Generation of cerebral organoids from human pluripotent stem cells. Nature Protocols 9, 2329–2340. https://doi.org/10.1038/nprot.2014.158

Lewis, John , Love in action, On Being with Krista Tippett, March 28, 2013 https://onbeing.org/programs/john-lewis-love-in-action/

Liu, Y., Li, X., Zhao, J., Tang, X., Tian, S., Chen, J., Shi, C., Wang, W., Zhang, L., Feng, X., Sun, M.-X., 2015. Direct evidence that suspensor cells have embryogenic potential that is suppressed by the embryo proper during normal embryogenesis. Proc Natl Acad Sci U S A 112, 12432–12437. https://doi.org/10.1073/pnas.1508651112

Looman, J., 1976. Biological equilibrium in ecosystems 1. A theory of biological equilibrium. Folia geobot. phytotax. 11, 1–21. https://doi.org/10.1007/BF02853312

Lucas, W.J., Groover, A., Lichtenberger, R., Furuta, K., Yadav, S.-R., Helariutta, Y., He, X.-Q., Fukuda, H., Kang, J., Brady, S.M., Patrick, J.W., Sperry, J., Yoshida, A., López-Millán, A.-F., Grusak, M.A., Kachroo, P., 2013. The Plant Vascular System: Evolution, Development and FunctionsF. Journal of Integrative Plant Biology 55, 294–388. https://doi.org/10.1111/jipb.12041

Maestroni L, Matmati S, Coulon S. Solving the Telomere Replication Problem. Genes (Basel). 2017;8(2):55. Published 2017 Jan 31. doi:10.3390/genes8020055

Majumder, R., Sutcliffe, B., Taylor, P. W., & Chapman, T. A. (2020). Microbiome of the Queensland Fruit Fly through Metamorphosis. Microorganisms, 8(6), 795. https://doi.org/10.3390/microorganisms8060795

Majidzadeh, H., Lockaby, B.G., Governo, R., 2017. Effect of home construction on soil carbon storage-A chronosequence case study. Environmental Pollution 226, 317–323. https://doi.org/10.1016/j.envpol.2017.04.005

Margulis, Lynn, *Symbiotic Planet: A New Look at Evolution*, Basic Books, 2008

Maturana, Humberto R.; Varela, Francisco J. (1972). Autopoiesis and cognition: the realization of the living. Boston studies in the philosophy and history of science (1 ed.). Dordrecht: Reidel. p. 141. OCLC 989554341

Mandelbrot, Benoit B. , *The Fractal Geometry of Nature*, WH Freeman, 1982

Marshall, C.R., Raff, E.C., Raff, R.A., 1994. Dollo's law and the death and resurrection of genes. Proc Natl Acad Sci USA 91, 12283. https://doi.org/10.1073/pnas.91.25.12283

Martial, C., Cassol, H., Charland-Verville, V., Pallavicini, C., Sanz, C., Zamberlan, F., Vivot, R.M., Erowid, F., Erowid, E., Laureys, S., Greyson, B., Tagliazucchi, E., 2019. Neurochemical models of near-death experiences: A large-scale study based on the semantic similarity of written reports. Consciousness and Cognition 69, 52–69. https://doi.org/10.1016/j.concog.2019.01.011

Martin, Betty and Robin Dalzen, *The Art of Receiving and Giving: The Wheel of Consent*, 2021

Meaney, M.J., 2001. Maternal care, gene expression, and the transmission of individual differences in stress reactivity across generations. Annu. Rev. Neurosci. 24, 1161–1192. https://doi.org/10.1146/annurev.neuro.24.1.1161

Milking Of The Murex Snail At Ventanas Beach, n.d. . Ballena Tales Magazine and Travel Guide. URL https://www.ballenatales.com/milking-of-the-murex-snail/

Mitteldorf, Josh and Dorian Sagan, *Cracking the Aging Code: The New Science of Growing Old and What it Means for Staying Young*, Flatiron Books, 2016

Morin, Jack. *The Erotic Mind: Unlocking the Inner Sources of Passion and Fulfillment*. Reprint edition. Harper Perennial, 2012

Nardou, R., Lewis, E.M., Rothhaas, R., Xu, R., Yang, A., Boyden, E., Dölen, G., 2019a. Oxytocin-dependent reopening of a social reward learning critical period with MDMA. Nature 569, 116–120. https://doi.org/10.1038/s41586-019-1075-9

National Geographic Society, *Beyond Earth: Mapping the Universe*. National Geographic, 2003

Nowotschin, S., Hadjantonakis, A.-K., Campbell, K., 2019. The endoderm: a divergent cell lineage with many commonalities. Development 146. https://doi.org/10.1242/dev.150920

Omidvarnia, A., Zalesky, A., Ville, D.V.D., Jackson, G.D., Pedersen, M., 2019. Temporal complexity of fMRI is reproducible and correlates with higher order cognition. bioRxiv 770826. https://doi.org/10.1101/770826

Ongaro, V., Leyser, O., 2008. Hormonal control of shoot branching. J Exp Bot 59, 67–74. https://doi.org/10.1093/jxb/erm134

Opinion: Archaea Is Our Evolutionary Sister, Not Mother [WWW Document], n.d. . The Scientist Magazine®. URL https://www.the-scientist.com/thought-experiment/opinion-archaea-is-our-evolutionary-sister-not-mother-64254

Pandele, Emily. "Intro to Quantum Superposition". https://www.linkedin.com/pulse/intro-quantum-superposition-emily-pandele?trk=public_profile_article_view

Paul, E.A., 2016. The nature and dynamics of soil organic matter: Plant inputs, microbial transformations, and organic matter stabilization. Soil Biology and Biochemistry 98, 109–126. https://doi.org/10.1016/j.soilbio.2016.04.001

Peña Ramirez, J., Olvera, L.A., Nijmeijer, H., Alvarez, J., 2016. The sympathy of two pendulum clocks: beyond Huygens' observations. Scientific Reports 6, 23580. https://doi.org/10.1038/srep23580

Perez-Garijo, Ainhoa & Steller, Hermann. (2015). Spreading the word: Non-autonomous effects of apoptosis during development, regeneration and disease. Development. 142. 3253-3262. 10.1242/dev.127878.

Peters, L.D., 2016. Heteropathic versus homopathic resource integration and value co-creation in service ecosystems. Journal of Business Research 69. https://doi.org/10.1016/j.jbusres.2016.02.033

Plants feel the force: How plants sense touch, gravity and other physical forces [WWW Document], n.d. . ScienceDaily. URL https://www. sciencedaily.com/releases/2011/10/111021125711.htm

Pritchard, W.S., 1992. The brain in fractal time: 1/f-like power spectrum scaling of the human electroencephalogram. Int J Neurosci 66, 119–129. https://doi.org/10.3109/00207459208999796

Proenca AM, Rang CU, Qiu A, Shi C, Chao L (2019) Cell aging preserves cellular immortality in the presence of lethal levels of damage. PLoS Biol 17(5): e3000266. https://doi.org/10.1371/journal.pbio.3000266

Puglia, M.H., Krol, K.M., Missana, M., Williams, C.L., Lillard, T.S., Morris, J.P., Connelly, J.J., Grossmann, T., 2020. Epigenetic tuning of brain signal entropy in emergent human social behavior. BMC Medicine 18, 244. https://doi.org/10.1186/s12916-020-01683-x

Quinn, J.P., Savage, A.L., Bubb, V.J., 2019. Non-coding genetic variation shaping mental health. Current Opinion in Psychology, Genetics 27, 18–24. https://doi.org/10.1016/j.copsyc.2018.07.006

Ramchandani, S., Bhattacharya, S.K., Cervoni, N., Szyf, M., 1999. DNA methylation is a reversible biological signal. Proc Natl Acad Sci U S A 96, 6107–6112

Rang, Ulla & Proenca, Audrey & Buetz, Christen & Shi, Chao & Chao, Lin. (2018). Minicells as a Damage Disposal Mechanism in Escherichia coli. mSphere. 3. 10.1128/mSphere.00428-18

Reference, G.H., n.d. What is noncoding DNA? [WWW Document]. Genetics Home Reference. URL https://ghr.nlm.nih.gov/primer/basics/noncodingdna

Rodgers, R.J., Irving-Rodgers, H.F., 2010. Formation of the Ovarian Follicular Antrum and Follicular Fluid. Biol Reprod 82, 1021–1029. https://doi.org/10.1095/biolreprod.109.082941

Saintillan, David et al, Extensile motor activity drives coherent motions in a model of interphase chromatin, Proceedings of the National Academy of Sciences (2018). DOI: 10.1073/pnas.1807073115 as reported in "DNA 'dances' in first explanation of how genetic material flows through a nucleus" by Thomas Sumner, Simons Foundation, https://phys.org/news/2018-10-dna-explanation-genetic-material-nucleus.html

Sanchez, P., Nehlin, L., Greb, T., 2012. From thin to thick: major transitions during stem development. Trends in Plant Science 17, 113–121. https://doi.org/10.1016/j.tplants.2011.11.004

Sánchez-Higueras, Carlos, Sol Sotillos, James Castelli-Gair Hombría, Common Origin of Insect Trachea and Endocrine Organs from a Segmentally Repeated Precursor, Current Biology, Volume 24, Issue 1, 6 January 2014, 76-81

Scheres, B., 2007. Stem-cell niches: nursery rhymes across kingdoms. Nat Rev Mol Cell Biol 8, 345–354. https://doi.org/10.1038/nrm2164

Schick, K., Verveen, A.A., 1974. 1/f noise with a low frequency white noise limit. Nature 251, 599–601. https://doi.org/10.1038/251599a0

Sheldrake, Merlin, *Entangled Life: How Fungi Make Our Worlds, Change Our Minds & Shape Our Futures,* Random House, 2021

Schmülling, T., Cytokinin, in Encyclopedia of Biological Chemistry (Second Edition), 2013, https://www.sciencedirect.com/topics/neuroscience/cytokinin

Science for Non-Scientists: Carbon Dating – Student Environmental Resource Center, n.d. URL https://serc.berkeley.edu/science-for-non-scientists-carbon-dating/

Seydoux, G., Braun, R.E., 2006. Pathway to Totipotency: Lessons from Germ Cells. Cell 127, 891–904. https://doi.org/10.1016/j.cell.2006.11.016

Shedge, R., Krishan, K., Warrier, V., Kanchan, T., 2021. Postmortem Changes, in: StatPearls. StatPearls Publishing, Treasure Island (FL)

Sheldrake, Rupert and D.H. Northcote, The Production of Auxin by Autolysing Tissues, Planta, Berlin (1968), 80, 227-236, https://www.sheldrake.org/research/plant-and-cell-biology/abstract-the-production-of-auxin-by-autolysing-tissues

Simard, Suzanne, *Finding the Mother Tree: Discovering the Wisdom of the Forest*, Allen Lane, 2021

Smith, Eric and Harold J. Morowitz, *The Origin and Nature of Life on Earth: The Emergence of the Fourth Geosphere*, Cambridge U. Press, 2016,

Stolarz M. Circumnutation as a visible plant action and reaction: physiological, cellular and molecular basis for circumnutations. Plant Signal Behav. 2009;4(5):380-387. doi:10.4161/psb.4.5.8293

Structural Biochemistry/Nucleic Acid/DNA/DNA structure - Wikibooks, open books for an open world [WWW Document], n.d. URL https://en.wikibooks.org/wiki/Structural_Biochemistry/Nucleic_Acid/DNA/DNA_structure

Sopinka, Natalie M et al. "Manipulating glucocorticoids in wild animals: basic and applied perspectives." Conservation physiology vol. 3,1 cov031. 23 Jul. 2015, doi:10.1093/conphys/cov031

Stubbendieck, R.M., Vargas-Bautista, C., Straight, P.D., 2016. Bacterial Communities: Interactions to Scale. Front Microbiol 7. https://doi.org/10.3389/fmicb.2016.01234

Su, Y.-H., Liu, Y.-B., Zhang, X.-S., 2011. Auxin–Cytokinin Interaction Regulates Meristem Development. Mol Plant 4, 616–625. https://doi.org/10.1093/mp/ssr007

Sundermier, A., n.d. The particle physics of you [WWW Document]. symmetry magazine. URL https://www.symmetrymagazine.org/article/the-particle-physics-of-you

Szendro, P., Vincze, G., Szasz, A., 2001a. Bio-Response to White Noise Excitation. Electro- and Magnetobiology 20, 215–229. https://doi.org/10.1081/JBC-100104145

Szendro, P, Vincze, G., Szasz, A., 2001. Pink-noise behaviour of biosystems. European biophysics journal : EBJ 30, 227–31. https://doi.org/10.1007/s002490100143

Tennessen, J. M., & Thummel, C. S. (2011). Coordinating growth and maturation - insights from Drosophila. *Current biology* : CB, 21(18), R750–R757. https://doi.org/10.1016/j.cub.2011.06.033

The Ancient Art of Natural Dye Purple, 2016. . ClothRoads. URL https://www.clothroads.com/the-ancient-art-of-natural-dye-purple/

The Eyes Have It: Researchers Can Now Determine When A Human Was Born By Looking Into The Eyes Of The Dead [WWW Document], n.d. . ScienceDaily. URL https://www.sciencedaily.com/releases/2008/01/080129201238.htm

The Mathemagicians' Guild, 2020. The Mandelbrot Set Explained. van der Voort, T.S., Mannu, U., Hagedorn, F., McIntyre, C., Walthert, L., Schleppi, P., Haghipour, N., Eglinton, T.I., 2019. Dynamics of deep soil carbon – insights from ^{14}C time series across a climatic gradient. Biogeosciences 16, 3233–3246. https://doi.org/10.5194/bg-16-3233-2019

Vieira, C., Evangelista, S., Cirillo, R., Lippi, A., Maggi, C.A., Manzini, S., 2000. Effect of ricinoleic acid in acute and subchronic experimental models of inflammation. Mediators Inflamm 9, 223–228

Wahlsten, Douglas. *Genes, Brain Function, and Behavior: What Genes Do, How They Malfunction, and Ways to Repair Damage.* Academic Press, 2019

Watkinson, S., 2000. Life after Death: The Importance of Salmon Carcasses to British Columbia's Watersheds. Arctic 53, 92–96

What Happens to the Brain After Death? [WWW Document], 2019. . News-Medical.net. URL https://www.news-medical.net/health/What-Happens-to-the-Brain-After-Death.aspx

Wilczek, Frank. Entanglement Made Simple, Quanta Magazine, 2016, https://www.quantamagazine.org/entanglement-made-simple-20160428/#

Wohlleben, Peter. *The Hidden Life of Trees: What They Feel, How They Communicate – Discoveries from A Secret World,* Greystone Books, 2016

Yano JM, Yu K, Donaldson GP, et al. Indigenous bacteria from the gut microbiota regulate host serotonin biosynthesis [published correction appears in Cell. 2015 Sep 24;163:258]. Cell. 2015;161(2):264–276. doi:10.1016/j.cell.2015.02.047 https://www.ncbi.nlm.nih.gov/pmc/articles/PMC4393509/

Yazar-Klosinski, B.B., Mithoefer, M.C., 2017. Potential Psychiatric Uses for MDMA. Clinical Pharmacology & Therapeutics 101, 194–196. https://doi.org/10.1002/cpt.565

Yong, E., 2012. Yeast suggests speedy start for multicellular life. Nature. https://doi.org/10.1038/nature.2012.9810

Yu, S.-M., Li, B., Amblard, F., Granick, S., Cho, Y.-K., 2021. Adaptive architecture and mechanoresponse of epithelial cells on a torus. Biomaterials 265, 120420. https://doi.org/10.1016/j.biomaterials.2020.120420

Made in the USA
Las Vegas, NV
21 February 2023

67843364R00152